THE FIRST TERM
A Study of Legislative Socialization

Volume 18, Sage Library of Social Research

SAGE LIBRARY OF SOCIAL RESEARCH

The First Term

A Study of Legislative
Socialization

Charles G. Bell
Charles M. Price

Preface by HEINZ EULAU

Volume 18
SAGE LIBRARY OF
SOCIAL RESEARCH

 SAGE PUBLICATIONS   Beverly Hills   London

96559

In appreciation to Totton J. Anderson

and

William Buchanan

Copyright © 1975 by Sage Publications, Inc.

All rights reserved. No part of this book may be reproduced or utilized in any form or by any means, electronic or mechanical, including photocopying, recording, or by any information storage and retrieval system, without permission in writing from the publisher.

For information address:

SAGE PUBLICATIONS, INC.
275 South Beverly Drive
Beverly Hills, California 90212

SAGE PUBLICATIONS LTD
St George's House / 44 Hatton Garden
London EC1N 8ER

Printed in the United States of America

International Standard Book Number 0-8039-0500-9(C)
0-8039-0501-7(P)
Library of Congress Catolog Card No. 75-11130

FIRST PRINTING

TABLE OF CONTENTS

96559

ACKNOWLEDGEMENT

Though difficult to stipulate precisely, the genesis of this book may be traced back to a seminar in legislative behavior taught by William "Buck" Buchanan at the University of Southern California where the authors first met. Professor Buchanan's avid interest in legislative behavior certainly "rubbed off" on the authors. We also want to acknowledge the early substantial help provided by Fullerton State University, which gave a semester's research leave to one of the authors. The National Science Foundation (NSF Grant 1870) provided long-term and essential financial support during most of the project. Finally, the Friends of the University (Fullerton) provided needed "last-minute" support.

Additionally, we are indebted to a number of colleagues who have read portions of the manuscript and offered many helpful suggestions: Malcolm Jewell, George Blair, and Bob Ross. In particular, we want to express our thanks to Mary M. Lepper whose careful reading and editing of the manuscript made a substantial addition to its quality. Thanks also to Al Sokolow who shared with the authors his data and ideas.

Of course, the research could not have been done without the cooperation of the Assembly class of 1966. They suffered patiently through the lengthy interviews, were articulate, candid, helpful, and good-natured about the enterprise. Obviously, without their assistance as well as that of their staffs, this book could never have been written.

Special thanks also go to Ardilla Yule, Betty Ackerman, Mary Childs, and Marcella Thomas, typists who were always most cooperative; and to graduate students Gerald Wright, James Garrity, Michael Boss and Richard Lepper.

Though we would like to shift the blame for any errors or wrongdoing to some of the above, we must admit that final responsibility for the substance of this book rests with the authors.

—C.G.B.
—C.M.P.

PREFACE

It has been my good fortune in the last twenty years or so to occupy a peculiarly favorable observational standpoint in matters of legislative study. In fact, it was exactly twenty years ago, though it seems only yesterday, that the group of scholars later known as "Wahlke et al." and properly so designated in the notes to this work first met to design the research subsequently brought together in *The Legislative System*. If I can contribute anything other than either benediction or remonstrance to the work of Professors Bell and Price, therefore, it is the kind of perspective that comes from kibitzing on legislative studies over a good many years.

In that perspective, I can say with some assurance that, of the hundreds of studies influenced in one way or another by *The Legislative System*, few are as venturesome as the research on legislators socialization inaugurated and now brought to fruition by Professors Bell and Price. There is always the dilemma in the social sciences whether to conduct one's research in a research tradition and call it "replication," or whether to deviate and break new ground (taking the risk of failure). If one "merely" replicates (though I happen to place great value on replicative research), there is always the suspicion that one has not the brains to do anything else. But if in the quest for originality one ignores the research tradition, there is always the danger that the hoped-for originality will only be old stuff in a new disguise. As Professors Bell and Price demonstrate, there is no necessary conflict between working in a research tradition and novel research development—misunderstandings of Thomas Kuhn's theory of scientific revolutions notwithstanding.

What makes research development so fascinating to the involved kibitzer is the tendency, over time, of relatively minor research interests to grow both intensively and extensively. The research by Professors Bell and Price is a case in point. It represents the convergence of a legislative research tradition that was reasonably well along by the late fifties and research on "socialization" that only then began to become a scientific concern in its own right. Although the four-state study conducted by Wahlke and his colleagues was the first to report on legislators' socialization in 1959, it was an incidental concern and limited to legislators' pre-office experience. In picking up this concern and extending it to within-role socialization, Professors Bell and Price are working in a research tradition and yet are extending the frontiers of knowledge.

The symbiosis of legislative and socialization research is all the more remarkable because, in 1966 or so, when they conducted their first-wave interviews, Professors Bell and Price did not have the benefit of the great amount of political socialization theory and relevant testing that had become available by the time they came to analyze their data and write up their findings. I am not aware of any other within-role or institution-set elite socialization study that probes as deeply as the present work, and certainly not of one that uses a quasi-experimental panel design, with a control group to boot.

Hopefully, future researchers will pick up where Professors Bell and Price leave off, for it is only too obvious that a one-state study conducted in one period with relatively few "cases" cannot be anything but suggestive, and that the validity of the propositions advanced here is necessarily problematic. Fortunately, Professors Bell and Price not only present their research methods and strategies in a way which should make replication or extension feasible; but they also outline alternative yet complementary models of elite socialization which transcend the limitations of their own data and make their book of genuinely theoretical interest beyond the particular research site. In linking legislative role analysis and socialization theory, Professors Bell and Price locate themselves in a present that connects past and future. That their work can have an impact on the next generation of researchers in this field, I do not doubt.

—Heinz Eulau

Chapter 1

LEGISLATIVE SOCIALIZATION

Introduction

It seems clear that the framers of the American Constitution perceived the legislative branch of our tripartite system as the main repository for the democratic and representative elements of American government. Certainly, the courts were not designed to be democratic or representative, and, indeed, they were constructed as bulwarks against these elements. Moreover, while the President is elected by the people and is, hence, the representative of all the people of the nation, or as Rossiter puts it, "the voice of the public,"[1] in fact, there are large elements of the population which are unrepresented no matter who the President is. However, owing to the large number of Representatives and Senators in Congress, nearly every conceivable minority is directly represented in this body. In sum, it is difficult to imagine a democratic and representative government without a legislature, but as any observer of American political history knows, our legislatures have often had great difficulty fulfilling their democratic and representative functions.

While a legislative system may be necessary for a viable democracy, the mere existence of a legislative body is not sufficient. There is no need here to retell the sad history of the trials and tribulations of our American legislative institutions. Suffice it to say, in the eyes of many—citizens, politicians, and political scientists—the courts and the executive have often appeared more responsible and responsive to the needs of the people than have the legislatures. It is not by accident that the Supreme Court's Baker v. Carr reapportionment decision preceded a nationwide resurgence of state legislative reform. In some states, the part-time amateur legislatures have been converted into full-time, professionalized legislatures while in most others increased staff and research support have enabled part-time legislators to better meet the needs of the people. Additionally, the potential for augmenting the representative nature of American state legislatures was also a derivative of the "one man, one vote" Baker v. Carr decision.

But the reforms and reorganizations are only half the story. It is the legislator, in the end, who makes or breaks the institution. His abilities and interests in government, his values and ambitions, and his skills as legislator will be the deciding factor. It is our purpose in this volume to examine the ways in which legislators learn how to do their tasks, what they bring to the job and what they learn from their job. In short, we are concerned with the subfield of political socialization commonly referred to as *elite political socialization,* or even more specifically, as *legislative socialization.*

SOCIALIZATION

Some years ago, Herbert Hyman defined an individual's socialization as the "learning of social patterns corresponding to his social position mediated through various agencies of society."[2] While one can trace interest in the study of political socialization back to Plato's *Republic,* and though many other political theorists have, since, discussed the topic generally, it would be fair to state that very little systematic, comprehensive attention has been paid to the subject until very recently. Perhaps the most significant pioneering effort in systematic political socialization research was Charles Merriam's landmark study, *The Making of Citizens,* published in 1931.[3] Unfortunately, Merriam's book received little attention at the time and did not serve as the springboard for other research efforts. In 1959, however, Herbert Hyman wrote his monumental *Political Socialization*. This volume, it seems, did serve to provide the stimulus for such an outpouring of research and publications that Fred Greenstein recently described the subject as a "growth stock."[4]

Interestingly, most political socialization research thus far has been devoted to the childhood years and the development of early political attitudes. Very little research effort has been devoted to the area of adult socialization. Thus, Jack Dennis, in an article considering the various areas of political socialization research, observed in 1968 that the study of elite political socialization was one of the least developed areas in the field, and little has been done since to require a change in Dennis' assessment.[5] Equally important, we know of no scholar in the field who would assert that adult political socialization is of little or no consequence. The political adult is not simply the child writ large. Recently, Donald Searing and his colleagues engaged in a systematic analysis of the linkage between childhood political socialization and adult issue attitudes and behavior. While they claim no definitive judgment on the matter, their work clearly suggests that political socialization research has too long ignored the adult years. They reasonably assert that:

> political socialization continues throughout the life cycle; that not all childhood learning influences adult behavior; and that, in dynamic modern societies, political attitudes are rarely transmitted unchanged from one generation to another.[6]

Earlier, Arnold Rose had suggested that, because of the complexity of modern industrial society, an individual simply could not learn enough during childhood to successfully cope with adult political life.[7] Richard Dawson and Kenneth Prewitt have contended that, while childhood political orientations persist into adult years, additional adult experiences will lead to the restructuring and redefining of one's political orientations.[8] Searing et al. have, however, gone farther than anyone else to date in suggesting how little linkage there is between the political child and political adult.[9] Clearly, the strength of the linkage between child and adult political orientations is still unknown. It may well be that it is less strong than commonly assumed. As a result, adult political socialization probably is of greater consequence in shaping adult political orientations than was previously supposed.

It is with this belief both in the importance of the legislative process in the American system and in a strong concern for better understanding of adult political socialization that we turn to the narrower study of legislative political socialization.

LEGISLATIVE SOCIALIZATION

Legislative socialization is, in a sense, a further extension and refinement of adult political socialization. The main thrust of legislative socialization studies centers on adaptation to the legislative arena, and how legislators' attitudes develop in response to a totally new adult political experience. Therefore, while this study considers the basic political socialization processes experienced by legislators prior to their immersion in politics, the major emphasis of our research concerns the period of time just prior to the election of a new legislator; and his or her subsequent experiences in the first years in the legislature.

Legislative socialization, to slightly misquote Gabriel Almond, might be defined as:

> the process of induction into the [legislative] culture. . . . Its end product is a set of attitudes, cognitions, value statements, and feelings—toward the [legislative system, its various roles and role incumbents]. It also includes knowledge of values affecting, and feelings toward the inputs of demands and claims into the system, and the authoritative outputs.[10]

Unfortunately, little is known about the specific details of legislative socialization. Though a number of scholars have extensively described the problems that new legislators face in gaining acceptance from their colleagues, particularly in Congress,[11] few social scientists have conducted any sort of systematic study of this phenomenon.[12]

Among the major findings of the few studies undertaken, Heinz Eulau and colleagues report that legislators' political socialization is not limited to the early childhood or teen years but may be shaped at almost any phase of the life cycle.[13] Another study by Prewitt, Eulau and Zisk found no significant association between the age of initial political socialization and legislative roles.[14] The clear *implication* of these two studies is that there does exist some substantial process of legislative socialization and that newly elected legislators do not come to the legislature fully equipped with the roles, attitudes, and values which they will subsequently hold. In a recent article, the authors of this volume delineated some of the various formal and informal agents of legislative socialization operating in the California Assembly.[15] Ronald D. Hedlund, in a penetrating examination of the Iowa legislature, reports an association between legislative experience and the development of some legislative roles.[16] In another earlier report, the authors found that representational role (style) appeared to be a product of both pre-legislative and legislative experience.[17] Aside from the authors' present longitudinal study of California assemblymen, there has been no similar systematic analysis of the legislative socialization process over time at the state level. With few exceptions, the other attempts to research this topic have been based on data gathered from incumbents at various times *after* their initial election.[18] Certainly, the data compiled in these various studies are fragmentary. However, there is general agreement that the socialization process greatly shapes and influences the activities of our state legislatures.

While state legislatures lack the substantial formal organizational structure of Congress, they do offer exceedingly interesting laboratories for learning about the socialization process. As Malcolm E. Jewell and Samuel Patterson point out, there must always be some way for new members to learn how they are expected to behave, what they can expect of others, the limits of these rules and roles, and the penalties for violation.[19] Moreover, because most state legislatures operate differently from Congress—meet less frequently, are less addicted to the seniority principle, have higher turnover rates, are not paid as well, have smaller staffs and less prestige—does not suggest the legislative socialization patterns at the state level will be any less important. In fact, because of the relatively high turnover and the lack of a seniority system, if state legislatures are to function well, they must socialize freshmen as quickly and effectively as possible.

Background

The genesis of this study came with the reapportionment decisions of the Courts in the early 1960s requiring state legislative bodies (both lower and upper houses) to reapportion themselves on a population basis. It was clear that the 1966 California elections would produce a bumper crop of freshman legislators who could, in most cases, be identified prior to their election. (Indeed, in the California State Senate there were only eighteen holdovers out of forty after the elections—though fourteen of the twenty-two newcomers had served previously in the Assembly.) In the Assembly, the impact of reapportionment was more profound: twenty-one Assembly seats out of eighty were vacated in a massive game of political musical chairs. In addition, one Assemblyman ran for statewide office, six retired, and one died in office. Thus, in all, there were twenty-nine open districts, where there was no incumbent running and where a freshman had to be elected. Thus, a reasonably large, predictable and identifiable data base for a socialization study was assured. As a result of the election, this data base was further enlarged from twenty-nine to thirty-three because of the defeat of several incumbents. In sum, there were thirty-three newcomers out of a total membership of eighty elected to the California Assembly in November 1966, and these legislators make up our freshman legislator sample.

The setting for this study is the lower house of the California legislature, the State Assembly. Over the last decade, no other state legislature has received as much critical acclaim as the California State Legislature. It has been ranked as the number 1 state legislature by any number of different studies.[20] Because of its reputation, the California Legislature has become the model for many other state legislatures.[21] Indeed, the California Legislature's professional tone makes it more comparable to Congress in some ways than to many of the other state legislatures. In any case, the California Legislature provides a useful mid-point between a highly structured, professionalized, full-time Congress and a host of nonprofessional, loosely organized part-time state legislatures.

THE FRESHMAN CLASS OF '66

Several legislative authorities have noted that members first elected in a particular year like the "class of 1954" or "1966" develop a certain esprit. Nor surprisingly, newcomers attending social functions together, learning "the ropes" at the same time, possessing similar backgrounds, getting elected on similar issues and facing the same sorts of personal crises, develop a certain bond. Though this bond does loosen somewhat after the member has served for a time in the legislature, it has some long-term importance. For example, this is how one veteran described his class:

> My class was the first one in which freshmen began to take an active role. Prior to that they were backbenchers. When I was first elected there were only 27 Republicans; the 11 freshmen Republicans had to carry the burden. We had to learn quickly.[22]

The California freshmen elected in 1966 soon developed a class pride and unity, but it appears that this sense of togetherness may have been somewhat stronger than with previous classes. There seem to be two major reasons accounting for this: first, the size of the class (thirty-three) necessitated that some of the new members take on important duties from the outset; second, this was the first group of legislators elected to the newly professionalized legislature. The voters had in November of 1966 passed Proposition IA which among other things gave the legislators a $10,000 pay raise and provided for unlimited sessions. Many of the freshmen had run anticipating the change. Senior legislators (as well as freshmen) suggested to the authors that the qualifications of the 1966 class far surpassed those of previous classes, partially, perhaps, because the potential salary increase attracted a new kind of candidate. This is how one prominent Democratic leader in the Assembly described it:

> With each new election I'm impressed by the group of newcomers. There's a great difference between those who have been elected in the last session or two and some of the old guard.[23]

Thus, the new class of 1966 was distinctive. From the outset, many of its members had an opportunity to play important roles in a legislative body which pays little attention to seniority. They had an opportunity to play important roles, in part, because there were not enough experienced, able, senior legislators to fill all the critical positions on key committees, in party posts, on select committees, or, as committee chairmen, vice chairmen or subcommittee chairmen. Equally important, many of these freshmen were able to play these roles. As a result, legislative socialization occurred so rapidly that by their second year in the legislature, most of the members of this class of '66 already considered themselves "experienced" (an exceedingly short apprenticeship!). In short, members of the class of '66 took pride in the qualifications of their members, of the positions they attained, and of the influence they quickly wielded in the legislature.

In most ways, the California freshmen elected in 1966 clearly were not similar to the state's adult population nor, for that matter, to many of the senior legislators. In terms of occupation, education, and sociopolitical skills, they were far from typical.

Not surprisingly, attorneys made up the largest portion of the occupational background of the freshman class.[24] All the freshmen had completed at least some college work, nearly all were college graduates, and many had completed some postgraduate work. Since the statewide median for school years completed by the white portion of the state's population 25 years old or older was 12.1, it is obvious that the freshmen Assemblymen had more extensive formal educational backgrounds than the average adult citizen, or, for that matter, than previous legislative classes.[25] Because, newcomers tend to be younger than senior members, it is not surprising that the freshman class of 1966 was youthful, but the proportion of very young legislators in this class was startling—twenty of the thirty-three freshmen (61%) were under forty. Racially, they reflected the state's diverse ethnic patterns to some extent: there were four black newcomers, one Oriental, and one foreign-born among the freshmen. Clearly, most underrepresented of the state's ethnic minorities was the Mexican-American community, which totaled approximately 12% of the state's population. (Chicano representation in the Assembly did not become significant until 1972 when six (7.5%) were elected to that body, three for the first time.) Another underrepresented sector of the state's adult population was women—only two members of the class were female. Freshmen tended to come from middle-class homes and backgrounds, though a few (for example, several of the black legislators) did come from lower-class backgrounds.

Lastly, members of the class of '66, on the whole, had become politically socialized at a somewhat earlier age and in a more intense fashion than have most other Americans. Class members were asked in an open-ended question when they had first become active in politics; six referred specifically to early childhood experiences. For example, one's mother had been a ward leader in Kansas City; another mentioned that he had grown up having relatives serving in the legislature; and another referred to the fact that he had been elected Patrol Boy Captain in grade school. Four legislators mentioned high school experiences, generally running for some class office. Seven stated they had become politically active in college in groups such as the Young Republicans and Young Democrats. Nine reported becoming active in the adult phase of their lives. Only five of the freshmen stated that they had become politically active in middle age or later. Most of these newcomers had had substantial adult political experience; they had worked on the average in about six campaigns prior to running their own. Nearly half (fifteen) had campaigned previously for political offices, including the County Board of Supervisors, the City Council, the school board, Congress, and the County Central Committees, and some had been elected. Over two-thirds (twenty-one) belonged to Republican or Democratic Party organizations or clubs prior to their successful campaign.

Our findings on this facet of socialization appear somewhat at odds with those of James Barber, who contends that most freshmen elected to the state legislatures arrive at state capitols without any prior political experience. Barber states, "Probably, a majority of state legislators enter that office without even having worked in their political party."[26] This described well the situation in Connecticut and many other states in 1959 and in California in 1957. But it is clearly not now the case in California, nor, we suspect, in other professionalized state legislatures. Of the thirty-one freshmen in our sample, only four stated that they had not worked for other candidates prior to their own candidacy. (Of the thirty-three freshmen elected in 1966, one refused to participate in the study and another had served several years earlier in the Assembly.) In short, this class had most of the formal educational, political, and social skills necessary to allow them to fit quickly and easily into the legislature. Before proceeding any further, however, a brief description of the California Legislature would be useful.

THE CALIFORNIA STATE LEGISLATURE: OLD IMAGE

Historically, the California State Legislature has been plagued by image problems similar to, if not greater than, most of the other American state legislatures. Part of the reason for its low rating can be attributed to the generally low esteem Americans have of politicians. For example, the stereotype of the Congressman—fat, elderly, cigar-chomping, verbose, and corruptible—can be easily transferred to state legislators. Moreover, at both the national and state levels, it is the executive branch (President, Governors, and their administrations) which exude the impression of action. Legislatures, at best, seem to react. However, state legislators face additional problems beyond that of the U.S. Congressmen, and these have helped further lower the image of state legislators.

Part of the image problem faced by state legislators hinges upon their low visibility. Generally, state legislatures tend to operate in relative obscurity. The only lapses in this pattern are the occasional messy scandals which do receive banner headlines and media attention. Indeed, some citizens might well be under the impression that this is the only "news" taking place in the state capitol. One of the reasons accounting for this low profile may be an artifact of the location of state capitols. Most state capitols were originally located in geographic mid-points within the states in order to ease the nineteenth-century commuting problems of legislators, to provide citizens of the state greater access to their state government and to protect rural farm interests. However, as Kenneth Palmer has noted, this means that state capitols tend to be located in rural farming centers far away from the major population centers of the urban states—in Albany, Springfield, Madison, Austin, Tallahassee, or Sacramento rather than New York City, Chicago, Milwaukee, Dallas, Miami, or San Francisco-Los Angeles.[27] The metropolitan press and the other local media of urban centers tend to devote most of their attention to critical national or international events—war, peace, inflation or depression, and the like—or to local activities such as whether municipal bus fares should be raised or storm drains built. Until recently, they gave little coverage to moribund state legislatures. What news (excepting scandals) there was of state government frequently seemed mundane or trivial and was often buried on the back pages of the paper—credentialling requirements for elementary school teachers, protection of mountain lions, or abolition of public pay toilets. While these issues were of interest to some, they were not usually the sort to elicit much widespread public attention. Hence, tucked away in the rural heartlands of the state, far from the metropolitan press, dominated by rural legislators, and hamstrung by archaic rules and procedures, state legislatures and state government were not seen by the public as being particularly responsive, innovative, or relevant.

Other major factors further contributing to the low status of American state legislatures, and California's in particular, were the low pay and incredibly inadequate working conditions. Originally, state legislative service was considered almost like jury duty. It was a citizen obligation—something that "good" citizens owed their government. Certainly, the prevailing sentiment was (and still is in many states) that state legislators should be given only a token payment for their services, more like an honorarium than a living wage. Most state legislatures had constitutionally limited biennial sessions. In terms of commitment, legislators were lawyers farmers, businessmen, and realtors first, and lawmakers only secondarily. There were almost no provisions for professional staff, and legislators had to rely on two prime sources for their information: lobbyists and the executive branch. Expertise was low and turnover high. In this type of setting, special interests could thrive and exert enormous leverage over legislators.

In California, the Southern Pacific Railroad and its allies literally ran the legislature during the latter part of the nineteenth and early part of the twentieth centuries through payoffs, bribes, and campaign contributions.[28] After a brief flurry of progressive reform efforts at the turn of the century, special interests again secured domination of state politics in the decades following. In the 1930s, the 1940s, and well into the 1950s, perhaps the most notorious lobbyist every to serve in Sacramento (or any state capitol), Artie Samish, representing a host of powerful, wealthy clients, dominated the legislative scene in California. Samish's power and influence became so legendary that they rivaled that of the Governor of California. Samish boasted that he paid his key staff more in a month's wages than legislators received for the entire year.[29] Through gifts, meals, call girls, campaign contributions, intelligence sources, and an intimate knowledge of the legislative process, Samish was able to completely control the actions of the California Legislature. Thus, while state legislators earned a pittance from their constitutionally limited salary, lived apart from their wives and families in Sacramento for several months every year, and, in general, had to live extremely frugally, many lobbyists lived sumptuously by comparison.

It is hardly any wonder that legislators were tempted by the largesse of the powerful lobbyists, with their generous expense accounts. When Lester Velie wrote his famed two-part series for *Collier's* in 1949 on "The Secret Boss of California," he described vividly and colorfully the extent of the corruption and control lobbyists and, in particular, Artie Samish, had over the legislature.[30] It would appear that Velie's disclosures merely reinforced what most of the California public had always thought: that California state government and the state legislature were hopelessly corrupt. Needless to say, the reputation of the California legislature has still not recovered completely from the Samish scandal or from other subsequent lobbyist-legislator indiscretions publicized in the press.

One further feature of the legislature during those years should be mentioned. During these earlier years, there was considerable opportunity for secrecy and "behind the scenes" manipulation of the legislative process. At executive sessions and dinner meetings of committees, no official committee voting records were kept, and legerdemain by chairmen was commonplace. Obviously, this feature further enhanced the ability of lobbyists to manipulate the process. Suffice it to say, the public's perception of the California legislature and politicians generally was not very high.

THE CALIFORNIA STATE LEGISLATURE: NEW IMAGE

Five major factors, frequently interacting and interrelating, have helped transform the California legislature from the institution it was into the type of institution it has become. The five factors are: (1) the development of heightened partisanship in the legislature; (2) the Supreme Court-ordered reapportionment based on the "one man, one vote" principle; (3) the development of a professionalized state legislature; (4) the decline of the powerful "old" lobbyists; and (5) structural changes and reforms within the legislature.

Partisanship. At the turn of the century in California, the progressives instituted a series of reforms aimed at reducing the influence of politicians and political machines in the state's political processes. Among the reforms were the adoption of civil service for state employees, nonpartisan local elections, prohibition on political parties making primary endorsements, and cross-filing, which was a device allowing candidates of one party to run in another party's primary. The partisan affiliations of the candidates were not included on the ballot. (In some years, a majority of incumbents won *both* major party nominations in the primary elections. Most, in their efforts to do so, ran "nonpartisan" campaigns.) In 1952, this procedure was modified and, in 1959, completely abolished. The modification of cross-filing in 1952 marks the beginning of a partisan trend in the legislature—particularly in the Assembly. Many Democratic legislators had for years felt that cross-filing was designed to rig the election process for the Republicans. In 1954, when for the first time voters were informed of a candidate's party affiliation in the primary election, a host of new Democrats were elected to the state legislature—including the man who later came to epitomize legislative partisanship, Jess Unruh. The new Democrats elected to the legislature and some of the older, veteran Democrats argued that the nonpartisan tradition of the legislature was a façade and that Republicans had actually dominated the process in a covert, partisan manner.[31] During this same period (1952-1954), the California Democratic Council was formed. It attempted to persuade Democratic legislators to support and vote for liberal Democratic positions in the legislature, as had the California Republican Assembly and later United Republicans of California urged Republican legislators to support the conservative Republican position.

First in the Assembly and then later in the Senate, party caucuses began meeting during this period to plan strategy, socialize, and attempt to seek common positions. In the Assembly by the

1960s, the Speaker increasingly came to be elected in the majority party caucus with the vote of the full Assembly being mere formal ratification. This was the case with the election of the last three Speakers, Jess Unruh, Robert Monagan, and Robert Moretti. In the 1960s, substantial professional staffs for both caucuses were also added. Proof of this heightened partisanship has been attested to by a number of different scholars doing roll call studies of the California legislature.[32]

Reapportionment. Another development which brought profound change in the California State Legislature followed the Supreme Court's reapportionment decision, Baker v. Carr, and the later extension of this decision in Reynolds v. Sims. The Court's ruling was implemented in California in the case of Silver v. Jordan (1965), and as a result the southern half of the state acquired an absolute majority of legislators in both houses. For years, the Assembly had been southern and urban in orientation, and the Senate had been northern and rural. Reapportionment brought the State Senate into conformity with population distributions—giving it, too, a substantial southern-urban-suburban flavor. Bruce Robeck contends that the growing partisan mood of the California Senate is directly linked with reapportionment, because the new districts tended to be more homogeneous and more clearly Republican or Democrat in orientation than the old county districts.[33]

Professionalization. Another significant change in the contemporary legislature from earlier days has been the extent to which the legislature has become professionalized. For many years, California has been in the vanguard of legislative reform in developing capable staff resources. Among such resources were: the Office of Legislative Analyst, to provide budgetary and fiscal advice to legislators; the Legislative Counsel, to provide bill-drafting resources for legislators; and the Auditor General, to keep track of spending in the different agencies. But it has only been in the last decade or two (some might argue since the Unruh era began) that the real development of staff came. Committee consultants, administrative assistants, the Office of Research, Caucus staff, and party leadership staff along with an extensive panoply of housekeeping staff—secretaries, sergeants, clerks, and interns—make up the best-staffed state legislature in the country. The physical resources of the California legislature have also become the envy of other state legislatures—committee hearing rooms, private individual office suites, and comfortable decor. Perhaps the most impressive changes have come in the personal life styles of legislators. Legislators today receive a $21,120 yearly salary which is not constitutionally limited. In addition, they receive $30.00 per diem, tax free, while the legislature is in session; have a car-leasing arrangement; are provided gas and telephone credit cards; receive funds for district office rent, postage, and mailers; and have a generous retirement system. There is little question that part of the reason for the high ranking of the California legislature by the several different studies evaluating state legislatures is because of the strides made by the California legislature in professionalization.

Lobby Decline. While there is considerable debate surrounding the issue of whether lobby influence has actually declined over the last few years, there is no question that the style of lobbying and the overt role that lobbyists play has changed. Part of the change can be related to the shocking Samish disclosures. At the time of the study, lobbyists had to register and report expenditures over $25. After 1974, the restrictions became much greater (see n. 34). Another part of the differences can be attributed to the changes previously discussed. Lobbyists flourished in the old nonpartisan days, where responsibility and accountability were often difficult to fix. Moreover, "old" style lobbyists often operated without much competition. There has been a great expansion in the number of lobbyists, including the new breed who represent the broad public interest. Lobbyists had influence in the old days because legislators were poorly paid, but this too has changed. Lobbyists probably exerted their greatest influence over the "old" rural Senate, but reapportionment has changed that chamber. The flamboyance and outright corruption of the old-style lobbyists seem today only part of a distant past. Legislators bring their families with them to Sacramento, and the old night-life social patterns of legislator-lobbyist have been sharply reduced. Instead of power being centered in lobby groups like the Derby Club (an eating group comprising senior legislators and well-heeled lobbyists) or the "Moosemilk" (another lobby eating group), it seems today to be centered in anti-lobby groups such as the "Micemilk" (a liberal Democratic luncheon group that "brown bags it," instead of relying on lobbyist money for meal tabs).[34] Finally, some legislators in their new-found independence, have used lobbyists—signing lobbyists' names to meal tabs, flooding them with "invitations" to testimonial dinners, and taking advantage of their hospitality in traveling about the state. Ironically, considerable pressure seems, today, to be directed *toward* the lobbyists! Given the large number of competing lobbyists and the reduced need for their information services (due to the large legislative staff), many lobbyists today are trying to get off the "hook." The recently enacted lobby reforms may do that.[3 5]

Procedural Changes. Lastly, a number of important and significant procedural changes have also been instituted over the past few years to help make the legislature operate more efficiently, effectively, and responsibly. Today the legislature conducts its business in two-year sessions, like Congress. Committee votes are now recorded. It would also seem that the legislature is more sensitive to the secrecy issue, and committees seem somewhat more reluctant to call executive sessions, particularly with an increasingly vigilant press following the proceedings.

The Challenge

The changes that have come about in the legislature and the reputation it has achieved nationally have brought about a new problem for the California legislature—expectations have exceeded results. There have been increasing stories in the press hinged around the theme: "Are we getting our money's worth?" The argument raised in the press is that, since we pay legislators well and staff and house them more than adequately, why do they "accomplish" so little? Criticisms have been raised over the legislature's inability to reapportion itself; resolve important issues such as welfare reform, tax issues, or health care; develop new programs; and over the use of staff members in election campaigns. Whatever the merits or demerits of these criticisms, there is little doubt that they are being raised persistently.

Thrust into the nation's most professionalized state legislature, the class of '66 displayed a high level of intelligence, energy, and ability to learn. In the following chapters, we shall describe and analyse this socialization process. What and how these freshmen Assemblymen learned is important not only to our understanding of legislative socialization but of the legislative process as well.

NOTES

1. Clinton Rossiter, *The American Presidency* (New York: Signet Key, 1956), pp. 22-23.

2. Herbert H. Hyman, *Political Socialization* (Glencoe: Free Press, 1959), p. 25.

3. Charles E. Merriam, *The Making of Citizens* (Chicago: University of Chicago Press, 1931).

4. Fred I. Greenstein, "A Note on the Ambiguity of 'Political Socialization': Definitions, Criticism, and Strategies of Inquiry," *Journal of Politics,* Vol. 32, No. 4 (November 1970), p. 969.

5. Jack Dennis, "Major Problems of Political Socialization Research," *Midwest Journal of Political Science,* Vol. 12, No. 1 (February 1968), p. 111.

6. Donald D. Searing, Joel J. Schwartz, and Alden E. Lind, "The Structuring Principle: Political Socialization and Belief Systems," *American Political Science Review,* LXVII (June 1973), p. 415.

7. Arnold M. Rose, "Incomplete Socialization," *Sociology and Research,* XLIV (March-April 1960), p. 244.

8. Richard Dawson and Kenneth Prewitt, *Political Socialization,* (Boston: Little Brown, 1969), pp. 204-205.

9. Searing, op. cit.

10. Gabriel Almond, "A Functional Approach to Comprative Politics," *The Politics of Developing Areas,* Gabriel Almond and James S. Coleman, eds. (Princeton: Princeton University Press, 1960), pp. 9 and 27-28.

11. Perhaps the leading exception to this general rule is James D. Barber, *The Lawmakers* (New Haven: Yale University Press, 1965). In this volume, Barber focuses on recruitment and adaptation problems of Connecticut legislators. He describes four different role typologies Connecticut legislators tend to play: the spectator, the advertiser, the reluctant, and the lawmaker.

12. Almost all of the basic texts on Congress and the state legislatures describe the freshman's problems of gaining acceptance from one's colleagues. Two of the more noteworthy explorations of this topic would be Charles W. Clapp's description of the House, *The Congressman: His Work as He Sees It* (Washington: Brookings Institution, 1963), and Donald Matthews' description of the Senate, *U.S. Senators and Their World* (New York: Random House, 1960).

13. Heinz Eulau, John Wahlke, William Buchanan, and LeRoy Ferguson, "The Political Socialization of American State Legislators," *Midwest Journal of Political Science,* III (May 1959).

14. Kenneth Prewitt, Heinz Eulau and Betty Zisk, "Political Socialization and Political Roles," *Public Opinion Quarterly,* XXX (Winter, 1966-67).

15. Charles M. Price and Charles G. Bell, "Socializing California Freshmen Assemblymen: The Role of Individuals and Legislative Sub-Groups," *Western Political Quarterly,* XXIII (March 1970), pp. 166-179.

16. Ronald D. Hedlund, "Legislative Socialization and Role Orientations," Laboratory for Political Research, University of Iowa, Report 11, October 1967. See also John C. Wahlke, Heinz Eulau, William Buchanan, and LeRoy Ferguson, *The Legislative System* (New York: Wiley, 1962), pp. 258-260.

17. Charles G. Bell and Charles M. Price, "Pre-Legislative Sources of Representational Roles," *Midwest Journal of Political Science,* XIII (May 1969).

18. James Barber's 1959 study of 150 Connecticut freshman legislators did employ a pre-session and post-session mailed questionnaire. The return rate was 55% and 64%,

respectively. In addition, he secured essentially unstructured interviews with 27 freshmen (18%). While a stimulating effort, it falls short of the systematic rigor required.

19.   Malcolm E. Jewell and Samuel C. Patterson, *The Legislative Process in the
United States* (New York: Random House, 1966), p. 20.

20.   The most useful volumes dealing with this topic are Calvin Clark, *A Survey of
Legislative Services in the Fifty States* (Kansas City, Mo.: Citizens' Conference on State
Legislatures, 1967), *American State Legislatures: Their Structure and Procedures*
(Chicago: Council of State Governments, 1967); and the Citizens Conference on State
Legislatures, *State Legislatures: An Evaluation of Their Effectiveness* (New York:
Praeger, 1971). Much of the discussion on this topic in this chapter is based upon data
from these sources.

21.   Particularly noteworthy in this regard, during the 1960s the then Speaker of the
California Assembly, Jess Unruh, was invited to speak before any number of state legislatures on the topic of professionalization.

22.   Interview with authors, February 21, 1968.

23.   Interview with authors, February 26, 1968.

24.   Dean McHenry reported that lawyers constituted about 35% of the legislators
during the 1930s. They made up 42% of the 1966 freshman class. "Legislative Personnel
in California," *Annals of the American Academic of Political and Social Sciences,* Vol.
195 (January 1938), pp. 48-49.

25.   McHenry, ibid., p. 47, found that only a slight majority of legislators serving in
the 1930s had attended college.

26.   James D. Barber, op. cit., p. 223. Barber cites data from other studies of New
Jersey, Ohio, Tennessee, California, and Missouri. The California data were based on a
survey conducted in 1957.

27.   Kenneth Palmer, *State Politics in the United States* (New York: St. Martin's
Press, 1972), p. 8.

28.   George E. Mowry, *The California Progressives* (Berkeley and Los Angeles: University of California Press, 1951), p. 12. For other excellent descriptions of this particular period, see Oscar Lewis, *The Big Four* (New York: Alfred A. Knopf, 1946); Richard
Harvey, "California Politics: Historical Profile," in *California Politics and Policies,*
Eugene P. Dvorin and Arthur J. Misner, eds. (Reading, Mass.: Addison-Wesley, 1966),
p. 76; Royce D. Delmatier et al., *The Rumble of California Politics* (New York: Wiley,
1970), chapter 6.

29.   Artie Samish and Bob Thomas, *The Secret Boss of California* (New York:
Crown, 1971).

30.   Lester Velie, "The Secret Boss of California," *Collier's,* Vol. 124 (August 13 and
20, 1949).

31.   See Royce P. Delmatier, "The Republican Party's California," and "The Rebirth
of the Democratic Party," op. cit., pp. 192-271. Also see Robert J. Pitchell, "The
Electoral System and Voting Behavior: The Case of California's Cross Filing," *Western
Political Quarterly,* Vol. 12, No. 2 (June 1959), pp. 459-84.

32.   Bruce W. Robeck, "Legislative Partisanship, Constituency and Malapportionment," *American Political Science Review,* Vol. LXVI, No. 4 (December 1972), pp.
1254-1255; and Charles M. Price, "Voting Alignments in the California Legislature: A
Roll Call Analysis of the 1957-1959-1961 Sessions" (unpublished Ph.D. dissertation,
Department of Political Science, University of Southern California).

33.   Robeck, ibid., pp. 1254-1255.

34. See Charles G. Bell and Charles M. Price, "Conflict and Consensus: The Development of Role Orientations and Ideology in Legislative Sub-groups," presented at the 1971 annual meeting of the American Political Science Association. In January 1975, the Derby Club was temporarily suspended pending clarification of new lobby controls enacted in Proposition 9 in June 1974.

35. In fact, one powerful lobby, the Santa Anita Racetrack, recently publicly announced that it would eliminate all direct contributions to legislators. Instead, the racetrack will provide campaign mailing services to *every* legislator via a computer mail firm. At the same time, legislators were informed that Santa Anita would make no other campaign contributions.

Chapter 2

LEGISLATIVE SOCIALIZATION MODEL

In this chapter, we attempt to construct a theoretical framework within which to analyze our data and present our findings. Several different kinds of factors had to be considered in the construction of the framework. First, we were concerned with what was learned; second, when it was learned; third, how it was learned; and fourth, the correlates of the learning process. Lastly, we wanted to present our findings in such a way that they could be integrated with other research, *most of which has yet to be done.* The following model is our attempt to resolve these needs in a relatively satisfactory way.

The Period-Phase Dimension

In time sequence, legislative socialization includes four separate time periods. The first period, *basic political socialization,* takes place in early childhood as the individual develops his basic political attitudes. values, beliefs, and the perceptions which are part of the citizenship preparation most Americans undergo.[1] Clearly, it is this period which socialization researchers have explored most extensively. The second period, *transitional political socialization,* occurs when one begins to participate actively in politics. While most citizens undergo at least a modicum of basic political socialization, only a few become political activists: working in campaigns, contributing money to the cause, walking a precinct, attending a party meeting, or, lastly, running for elective office. For our purposes, the first two periods will be called the *preparatory legislative socialization* phase—i.e., those periods which take place prior to a person's officially becoming a member of the legislature (the "before" phase).

The third period, *initial legislative socialization,* takes place approximately during one's first term in the legislature. In this period, the political attitudes, values, beliefs, and expectations which the new legislator brings from his or her previous life experiences are complemented, modified, or perhaps altered by legislative experiences. In this period, the various legislative socializing forces, both individual and group, help orient the new legislator to the job. It is our contention that the experiences of this period have a profound impact on the lawmaker's future career. The fourth period, *secondary legislative socialization,* is entered as the new legislator becomes accepted (or gets rejected) by colleagues, loses the neophyte status, and possibly begins to take a leading role in committee, on the floor, or in caucus. Since the third and fourth periods, unlike the first two, are specific to the job of being a legislator, we have identified the latter two periods as the *specific legislative socialization* phase (the "after" phase).

Our concept of preparatory legislative socialization owes much to Hess and Torney, Dawson and Prewitt, and Barber.[2] Hess and Torney, in their study of childhood political socialization, discuss at some length preparation for adult politics.

> It seems useful to think of this [socialization] process as one which has both upward reference to agents (like parents, teachers), lateral references to peer groups, and chronological or longitudinal reference to a future time and status when present socialization may have its most direct application. From this last perspective, socialization anticipates the adult behavior with which it is concerned, preparing the individual for a role which he will exercise more completely at some later time.[3]

They refer to this as "anticipatory," which we feel would be mis-leading for our purpose, since very few people anticipate playing the legislative role. Dawson and Prewitt, in their work, refer to this process as "indirect."[4] In their discussion of indirect political socialization, they, too, lean heavily upon Hess and Torney. Almond and Verba perhaps sum up the process as well as anyone:

> The role that an individual plays within the family, the school, or the job may be considered training for the performance of political roles. ... Participation in non-political decision-making may give one the skills needed to engage in political participation, the skills of self-expression and a sense of effective political tactics.[5]

Broadly speaking, the preparatory legislative socialization phase includes the acquisition of values prior to their being opera-tional. It also deals with the learning and practicing of social skills generally applicable to a wide range of social and interper-sonal transactions which may also be specifically applicable to a political situation.

An illuminating and well-known example of preparatory legis-lative socialization is the occupational training and experience of the lawyer. (One of the notable political facts of life is that attorneys constitute a disproportionately large segment of most legislative bodies.) Perhaps some young men or women enter legal training with an eye on the state capitol, but, for all of them, the training and experience of the lawyer are an obvious preparation for the job of lawmaker.

The specific legislative socialization phases take place after the member has been sworn in. The first year, in particular, appears to be a time of intensive and extensive efforts by fresh-men to acquire the knowledge needed to be a successful legis-lator.[6] During the first months, a new legislator is socialized and integrated by veteran legislators, lobbyists, members of executive branch, and many others. Recent studies by Alan Fielin, Stephen V. Monsma, and by the authors provide substantial insight into this process.[7] In the latter two periods, we shall explore exten-sively the impact membership makes on legislators' perceptions, values, expectations, and role orientations. Particularly in the secondary legislative socialization period, we will consider why some legislators are given choice assignments and others are not, and we shall also consider why some legislators are viewed as "effective" by their colleagues while others are not.

Admittedly, the periods and phases described overlap to an extent and are not always clear-cut; however, we feel they are distinctive enough to help provide a convenient framework for analyzing legislative socialization. In short, though the boundaries separating one from another are not always precise, we are confident that nearly all legislators go through these four periods (for a more elaborate discussion of this, see Chapter 7).

The Process Dimension

The second dimension of our model is one of process. We have used the process models developed by Hess and Torney in their study of childhood political socialization and experimentally adapted them for use in our study of legislative socialization.[8] Briefly, these models are:

(1) The "accumulation model" sees political socialization as a direct learning process;

(2) "interpersonal transfer model" sees the application of knowledge already held applied to a new situation;

(3) "identification model" sees the individual imitating the actions, values, or roles of some significant other; and

(4) "cognitive-developmental model" assumes that the capacity to handle concepts and information sets limits on the understanding that can be acquired of the political process.

An example of the accumulation model can be seen in the child learning about the structure of state government in a civics class; or, perhaps, the young adult who, in learning parliamentary procedure, also acquires an understanding of the principles of debate and political strategy. A specific example of the interpersonal model might be the learning of some of the informal rules of the game in school, community, or work groups. The techniques necessary to get along with people in formal group situations, such as the Kiwanis or Rotarians, may be similar to the legislature. The identification model can be found in operation when the child, imitating father, identifies with his or her father's political party.

Later, as an adult, one may take the same community activity role as an admired leading citizen, or a freshman legislator may consciously imitate a more senior lawmaker. Finally, the cognitive-developmental model is, in fact, the antithesis of the accumulation model. The cognitive-developmental model suggests that there are limits on each individual's capacity to learn. These limits are set not only by basic intellectual capacities, but, perhaps even more significantly, by each individual's values and concepts. Thus, it is hard to imagine someone with a self-image of failure ever seriously seeking election to the legislature, much less being an effective member of such a body. Similarly, it is also hard to visualize a legislator with a rigid value system engaging easily in the expected legislative process of compromise. (It is not hard to see him being elected, however.)

The Phase-Process Model

Combining the phase and process models produces a four-by-four heuristic matrix which specifies both time and type of legislative socialization. Figure 2.1, illustrates this. Thus, the process of accumulation may be found during any of the four periods. Or, conversely, within the initial legislative socialization period one may find all four processes. For example, the freshman legislator learning the mechanics of the consent calendar illustrates the accumulation process during the initial legislative socialization period. Or, in considering the interpersonal transfer model, Dawson and Prewitt's discussion of apprenticeship seems to apply.

> Non-political activities are viewed as practice or apprenticeship for political activities. From various non-political experiences the individual acquires skills and insights which he uses to find his way in the political world.[9]

Learning how to work with people as a member of a civic organization is an obvious example. Apprenticeship is a meaningful term in the sense of the learning of occupational skills and roles, and appears to have considerable applicability, particularly in legislative bodies.

In evaluating our model of legislative socialization, one might assume that a similar process takes place in medical school, law

Process:	Phases			
	Preparatory Legislative Socialization Phase		Specific Legislative Socialization Phase	
	Basic Socialization Period	Transitional Socialization Period	Initial Legislative Socialization Period	Secondary Legislative Socialization Period
Accumulation				
Interpersonal				
Identification				
Cognitive-Developmental				

Figure 2.1: A PHASE-PROCESS MODEL OF LEGISLATIVE SOCIALIZATION

school, apprenticeship for journeyman plumber, or any one of a number of occupational situations. A word of caution is therefore in order. As Heinz Eulau and associates have suggested, for most state legislators, a political career is only a part-time occupation at best. Neither the time spent as a legislator nor the salary is sufficient to exact the same level of job commitment that most occupations call for.[10] As we have indicated in the previous chapter, the time and effort devoted to the job of legislator is not great in many states. James Barber's study of Connecticut freshmen illustrates this point. Using his unique role typology of "spectator," "advertiser," "reluctant," and "lawmaker," Barber found that one-third of the freshman legislators were not anxious to be re-elected, while another third, the "spectators," were generally passive members of the body.[11] At the time of Barber's study (1957) the Connecticut legislature was a typical part-time amateur body. (Like many other amateur legislatures, Connecticut's has also moved toward professionalization. As of 1973, the General Assembly met every year, and legislators were paid a two-year total of $10,106 in salary and up to $2,000 in expenses. In addition, the Assembly has hired professional staff to service both houses.)

Meeting every other year, paid an average of $2,000 per year in salary and expenses, lacking offices and provided with minimal secretarial assistance, they clearly could not be expected to make a full-time commitment to the job. While the difference between states is more likely one of degree than of kind, it is a difference which must be considered. But, ironically, it is in states like California, where the socialization process is likely to be more intense, that the researcher has the best opportunity to study the phenomenon with his often insensitive instruments.

Research Methodology

PANEL DESIGN

In order to better understand how the legislative socialization process operates, we decided the most useful technique would be a "before and after" survey design. Eventually, this meant interviewing the same respondents three separate times: first, before they had had any experience as legislators; second, after approximately one year's service in the legislature; and, third, during the first part of their second term (see Figure 2.2). The assumptions of such a design were: (1) data gathered during the first interviews are the result of pre-legislative experience; (2) data gathered during the subsequent interviews are partially the result of the intervening variable of legislative experience; and (3) it is possible to sort out the impact of such legislative experience. Additionally, another set of interviews was conducted with thirty-four (71%) of the veterans. The veterans' interviews provided additional data which help facilitate the analysis of the legislative socialization process. (A more detailed and extensive discussion of the research design—limitations of the panel approach, problems of measuring change, identifying freshmen, and discussion of interview questions—will be found in Appendices.)

Hypotheses

Our first major hypothesis was that legislative role orientations would be substantially the product of prior life experiences, and, as a result, legislative service would not substantially change orien-

	Before Legislative Experience		After One Years Legislative Experience		After Two Years Legislative Experience	Bench Mark
Interview	I (1966)		II (Winter 1967-1968)		III (Spring 1969)	V (1969)
Respondents	Potential Freshmen		Freshmen With One Years Experience		Freshmen Starting Second Term	Veterans
Data Gathered	Personal Past Political Rules of the Game Roles Input Perceptions Interest Group Knowledge		Rules of the Game Roles Input Perceptions Interest Group Knowledge Legislative Effectiveness Legislative Group Membership Press Relations Work Load Expertise Development		Rules of the Game Roles Input Perceptions Legislative Effectiveness Legislative Group Membership	Rules of the Game Roles Input Perceptions Legislative Effectiveness Legislative Group Membership

INTERVENING VARIABLE — SERVES IN ASSEMBLY ONE YEAR

INTERVENING VARIABLE — SERVES IN ASSEMBLY TWO YEARS

Figure 2.2: THE PANEL DESIGN

tation. Some of the minor hypotheses developed from the major hypothesis were:

(1) Representational role orientations of legislators are largely the product of life experience prior to legislative service.

(2) Interest group role orientations of legislators are largely the product of life experience prior to legislative service.

(3) Party role orientations of legislators are largely the product of life experiences prior to legislative service.

Role orientations were measured by using batteries of agree-disagree scale items taken largely from the earlier work of Wahlke et al. In one instance, an item was added, while in a few others words were slightly changed or added to suit our particular needs. The advantage of using the Wahlke items was not only in their susceptibility to statistical manipulation, but to the fact that there has been a substantial body of work based on them subsequent to publication of *The Legislative System*.[1][2] This was particularly important since California was one of the states included in *The Legislative System.*

Our second major hypothesis was that freshman legislators who were knowledgeable and familiar with the "rules of the game" prior to their legislative experience would be in a position to rise more rapidly within the ranks of the Assembly than would their less-prepared colleagues. Some of the minor hypotheses developed from the major hypothesis were:

(1) Legislators-to-be with prior legislative experience (city council, board of supervisors, or school board) would be more knowledgeable of the rules of the game than those with no such prior experience.

(2) Education would be positively associated with knowledge about the rules of the game.

(3) Political experience in campaigns or membership in a political club would be positively associated with knowledge of the rules of the game.

(4) Activity with community/civic organizations would be positively associated with knowledge of rules of the game.

Knowledge and attitudes about the rules of the game were measured by several questions, one of which was scaled. Essentially, however, we asked open-ended questions in an attempt to see what aspiring legislators knew about the rules of the game. In this way, too, potential legislators were not given any clues as to what some of the rules might be. Here again, we drew heavily upon the work of Wahlke et al. and Kornberg.[13]

The third major hypothesis considered in this volume is that freshman legislators' perceptions of the significance of various legislative "input" factors would become more like veterans' perceptions over time. Several of the "input" factors have traditionally been considered to be sources of cohesion or conflict with legislative bodies. Some of the minor hypotheses included:

(1) Party would be associated with assessments of the significance of the bureaucracy in the legislative process.

(2) Northern freshmen would assess sectionalism as being less significant in the legislative process than would southern freshmen.

(3) Ideology would not be related to assessments of significance of legislative input factors.

Assessments of the significance of various "input" factors were obtained by using a seven-point self-anchoring scale ranging from not significant (0) to very significant (6). For each input factor—such as the "speaker" or "committee chairman"—the respondent was asked to indicate on the scale how important he thought each was in the legislative process. Use of the scale enabled us not only to measure changes over time but to calculate correlations with other variables such as ideology (a scale variable, too) or party (a dichotomous variable).

Finally, we have attempted to describe the many kinds of individual and group situations which are an integral part of the legislative socializing process. Information about the various "socializing groups" and about friendships was obtained through open-ended questions asked during the second and third interviews. Respondents were asked about the groups that existed, which they were active in, and who else were members. In this way, we were able to construct a crude model of a legislative group interaction system. We were also better able to understand and describe the many different agents of legislative socialization.

LIMITS

Institutional. Perhaps the most important limiting feature of this study is that it focused on *one* chamber of one state legislature, the California Assembly. While the California legislature is comparable to most other state legislatures in that it is bicameral, partisanly elected, and selects its own leadership, it also has unique features. At the time of our study (1966-1969), it was becoming the most professionalized of the state legislatures; it was also somewhat less partisan than many of the other large urban states; while lobbyists and special interests exerted an influence over its politics that *may have been* more extensive than in many of the other states, it was also in the process of substantial and rapid change. It probably is true that each of the fifty state legislatures has special or unique qualities distinguishing it from others, but overall many seem to be moving in the direction California has moved—toward a more professionalized legislature. (Indeed, by 1975, New York's state legislators, with their recent pay increase, will be earning several thousand dollars more a year than California's!)

Cohort. Our study focuses on one particular class, the class of '66, which was elected soon after the court-ordered reapportionment. The size of the freshman class (41% of the total legislative membership) and the almost inevitable significance played by these new members in the Assembly deliberations were certainly different from more normal years. Large turnover, a factor in some state legislatures, has not generally occurred in California in recent years.

Methodology and Theory. As was stated previously, one of the major problems faced by the authors in doing this research was that there were few systematic, comprehensive data from other studies that we could use to build upon or replicate in our own study. Hence, our theoretical phase-process model formulation was developed while we were gathering our data, conducting our interviews, and wrestling with our statistical problems. It would have been helpful to have had a fully developed theoretical model prior to our initial survey and questionnaire design (1965-1966) so that the analysis might have been congruent with the major works in the field. In 1965, this was not possible.

At that time, much of the work now considered basic in the field was not in print—Hess and Torney, Dawson and Prewitt, Dawson's bibliographic essay, Dennis' "Major Problems" article, and Easton and Denis, for example. Additionally, we would have liked to have been able to identify and interview all potential freshman legislators prior to their initial filing for office (February 1966) or at least prior to the primary election in June 1966. This was not possible either. Time, distance, and the great number of candidates prevented our attempting this. (Three hundred forty-three potential freshmen ran in the primaries.)

Conceptual. Another kind of problem should be kept in mind, too. After four sets of interviews (conducted by the authors—146 interviews in all, totalling 134 hours); countless hours spent in legislators' offices, committee rooms, in the Assembly chamber and in legislators' field offices; and after many conversations with Assembly staff, the authors are convinced that interview data fail in many ways to accurately define, assess, and express the *total reality of the legislature.* This is not to say that such data are inaccurate, but that they get at only certain aspects of the legislator's life. No doubt this same limit would apply to any similar study of attorneys, doctors, or college professors. Nor is this limit inherent only within the interview format. The totality of a given experience simply surpasses the ability of the social scientist to define, describe, or to measure it. This is certainly not an argument against the scientific method, but it is a recognition of the limits of our knowledge. Norwithstanding these limitations, the authors believe that the phase-process model of legislative socialization that we have formulated and the findings from our data help provide insights and understanding of the legislative socialization process not only in the California Assembly but in other American legislatures as well.

NOTES

1. We do not mean to imply that all American citizens learn to participate in the classic democratic sense. A number of studies have shown that a significant segment of the population learns not to participate or to participate in deviant ways. See Dean Jaros et al. "The Malevolent Leader: Political Socialization in an American Sub-culture," *American Political Science Review,* LXII (June 1968), pp. 564-575.

2. Robert D. Hess and Judith V. Torney, *The Development of Political Aptitudes in Children* (Chicago: Aldine, 1967) pp. 6-7; Richard E. Dawson and Kenneth Prewitt, *Political Socialization* (Boston: Little, Brown, 1969), pp. 65-73; and James David Barber, *The Lawmakers* (New Haven: Yale University Press, 1965), pp. 219-225.

3. Hess and Torney, op. cit., p. 6.

4. Dawson and Prewitt, op. cit., p. 65.

5. Gabriel A. Almond and Sidney Verba, *Civic Culture* (Boston: Little, Brown, 1965), pp. 327-328.

6. Herbert B. Asher, "The Learning of Legislative Norms," *American Political Science Review,* LXVII, (June 1973), pp. 499-513. Asher contends that freshmen members of Congress learned little in the way of norms during this first year. Newcomers evidently came to Congress aware of the norms. Indeed, Asher argues that veteran legislators, for the most part, give much *less* credence to the apprenticeship principle than do the freshmen! It is likely that most freshmen Congressmen come to Congress better prepared and more politically experienced than the typical newly elected state legislator.

7. Alan Fielin, "The Function of Informal Groups in Legislative Institutions: A Case Study," *Journal of Politics,* XXIV (February 1962), p. 72; Stephen V. Monsma, "Integration and Goal Attainment as Functions of Informal Legislative Groups," *Western Political Quarterly,* XXII (March, 1969), p. 19; and Charles M. Price and Charles G. Bell, "Socializing California Freshman Assemblymen: The Role of Individuals and Legislative Sub-groups," *Western Political Quarterly,* XXIII (March 1970).

8. See Hess and Torney, op. cit., pp. 19-20.

9. Dawson and Prewitt, op. cit., p. 69.

10. Heinz Eulau et al., "Career Perspective of American Legislators," in *Political Decision Makers,* Dwaine Marvick, ed. (New York: Free Press, 1961), p. 247.

11. James D. Barber, op. cit., pp. 24, 70, 118.

12. In addition to John Wahlke et al., *The Legislative System* (New York, John Wiley, 1962), see Kenneth Prewitt, Heinz Eulau, and Betty Zisk, "Political Socialization and Political Roles," *Public Opinion Quarterly,* XXX, No. 4 (Winter 1966-1967); Wayne L. Francis, "The Role Concept in Legislatures," *Journal of Politics,* XXCII, No. 3 (August 1965); Allan Kornberg, *Canadian Legislative Behavior* (New York: Holt, Rinehart & Winston, 1967); or Ronald D. Hedlund, "Legislative Socialization and Role Orientations," Laboratory for Political Research, University of Iowa, Report 11, October 1967.

13. Wahlke et al., op. cit.; Kornberg, op. cit.; and Allan Kornberg, "The Rules of the Game in Legislative Politics: A Comparative Study," *Journal of Politics,* XXVI (May 1964).

Chapter 3

AGENTS OF SOCIALIZATION

The socialization process which transforms private citizens into legislators is as complicated as it is critical. Unlike most groups, legislatures have little control over the composition of their membership. There is no blackballing of candidates, no matter how obnoxious a particular individual might be. If one wins election, he or she becomes a member. Therefore legislatures, if they are to function, must socialize their new members, not just educating them to the rules of the game but instilling in them a feeling of belonging.

Background

Several decades ago, Garland Routt observed, "The esprit de corps displayed by legislative bodies, especially the smaller ones, is probably not rivaled by any other formally organized self-governing body."[1] Certainly, what Routt described generally about legislatures can be said in particular about the California Assembly. It

AUTHORS' NOTE: This chapter has been significantly revised from an earlier presentation of the topic in the *Western Political Quarterly,* March 1970.

has only eighty members, and these members have common interests, loyalties, and a sense of union. They are proud that they have been elected to serve in the legislature and are aware of the considerable responsibilities this entails.

The pride, loyalty, and sense of union which are characteristics of legislators in general, and of California Assembly members in particular, are generated by several factors. In California, the eighty legislators of the Assembly are the final winners in a contest that once numbered hundreds of candidates and potential candidates, and thousands of voters. Each of the eighty has gone through the rigors of campaigning for office, getting nominated, and winning election. It is not surprising that a certain pride and camaraderie should develop among the eighty successful Assembly members. In addition, their pride is derived from the fact that California legislators have considerable prestige and influence. Decisions rendered by the legislature have far-reaching consequences for the entire state population.

Legislators in the California Assembly also take particular pride in pointing to the fact that many of the reforms pioneered in the California state legislature are just now being considered for adoption in other state legislatures. The most unique feature of the California legislature is the extent to which professional staff has been acquired. For many years, California legislators have been able to rely on the staff of the Legislative Council's office for bill-drafting duties; the Legislative Analyst's Office for fiscal expertise; and the Auditor-General for expertise in agency spending. However, in the early 1960s, the professionalization movement really flowered in the state legislature. Led by former Speaker Jess Unruh and a bipartisan coalition of legislators, the staff was greatly expanded to include administrative assistants, an office of research, committee consultants, majority and minority party consultants, leadership staff, and an augmented clerical component. In 1966, Unruh directed the successful Proposition 1A campaign which further accelerated the professionalizing trend already under way—legislators' salaries were raised, legislators were released from constitutional fetters in setting their salaries, and the legislature was given unlimited annual sessions. Today, California state legislators receive $21,120 yearly, plus $30.00 per diem when the legislature is in session. In short, California legislators earn approximately $27,000 per year.[2]

Besides their substantial pay and per diem, California Assembly members have a number of other perquisites of office, including handsome office suites, district offices, state cars, gasoline and telephone credit cards, secretarial pools, and travel allowances. In sum, though there are improvements which could be made, the California Assembly has most of the accoutrements of a modern, professional legislature. Thus, in addition to the normal institutional pride characteristic of most legislators, most California Assembly members also take considerable pride in the fact that this chamber has become a model for other state legislatures. When one compares the considerable support facilities enjoyed by California legislators with those available (and not available) in other states, it is clear that the California legislator is probably a part of the most professionalized state legislature in the United States.[3]

Indeed, the leaders of the Assembly became so concerned with conveying the proper professional image to the public that they instituted a number of reforms in the 1957 session. No longer were reporters given the run of the floor to conduct interviews with members. All Assembly members—particularly freshmen— were apprised of the importance of punctually attending sessions, not reading newspapers at their desks, and not leaving until adjournment. Off the floor, in committee hearings, attendance of members was checked carefully by the Speaker Pro Tempore. In fact, the emphasis on decorum was so severe that even most of the traditional floor hazing of freshmen was discontinued.[4] However, the practice of hazing freshmen was revived to some degree in the 1971 session.

Pre-Session Socialization

By the time we had conducted our first series of interviews with the potential freshmen of the class of '66 (months prior to their arrival at the state capitol), they had passed through the first period of "basic political socialization"—i.e., the period of heightened political activity. Each of our interviewees had made the decision to file for the Assembly; each had successfully weathered the June primary; and each was preoccupied with the details of planning the fall campaign.

For some, particularly for those who were shoo-ins in the fall election, the transition to period three, "initial legislative socialization," was already well under way. Money flowed into their campaigns from election committees set up by the parties in the Assembly, and many were already thinking of committees they wanted to or could hope to serve on, or the leaders they would be electing at the Republican and Democratic Party caucuses. Special candidate schools were conducted in Sacramento by legislative staff and other professionals to instruct the legislative aspirants in the organization and planning of their campaigns. Both parties attempted to marshall their greatest efforts in terms of campaign staff assistance and financial aid for candidates who had the best chance of winning. As a result, candidates who had the "best" districts were most exposed to pre-legislative socialization.

After the November election, both parties traditionally hold pre-session caucuses, whose prime purpose is to elect party leaders for the coming session and to consider party legislative strategy. (With the passage of Proposition 4 in 1972, sessions run two years. The effect on leadership selection is uncertain.) In some years, when the leadership in the Assembly Republican or Democratic ranks is secure, the pre-session caucus is a mere formality. Not infrequently, however, there is a struggle for leadership within party ranks; and freshman legislators, who often have relatively loose commitments to particular party leader candidates, are courted zealously for support. (Some of this courting occurs prior to the November elections.) For example, during the election campaigns (prior to selection as Speaker), Speakers Jess Unruh and Robert Moretti were active in raising money for needy Democrats. It has been suggested that the obligations and good will that accrued to these two leaders gave them a decisive advantage in later intraparty fights.

Obviously, the stakes for a freshman in this internal struggle are high, particularly if his or her party commands a majority in the Assembly. Over the last decade or two, the Speaker has, to all intents and purposes, been selected by the majority party caucus. Having supported the "right" man in the caucus and being part of his coalition is most advantageous to a freshman concerned with the disposition of bills and appointment to desired committees. The Speaker of the California Assembly selects all committee chairmen and all but one committee's members. The single exception is the Rules Committee. He also assigns all bills to committee.

Freshman members of the minority have different problems. They must elect a minority party leader who admittedly, has far less power than the Speaker. Of course, another decision faced by freshmen minority party members (and veterans as well) is what they should do on the formal speakership vote. The pattern has been that the majority party sticks together on this vote, and there is little real role for minority party legislators to play. There is, it is true, always the possibility that a losing speaker's faction of the majority party would refuse to support the caucus candidate and seek an alliance with the minority party to secure the forty-one votes necessary, but this does seem increasingly remote. In some instances, minority party members have voted for the majority party caucus candidate because of the inevitability of his election, because of a sense of legislative camaraderie and good will, or perhaps in hopes of gaining positions on good committees. But in doing so, they may incur the enmity of their own party leaders. In some instances, minority party members have abstained, while in other instances, they have continued to vote for their own minority party leader.

Lobbyists also try to build early good relationships with potential legislators, and thus serve as socializing forces. Prior to election they sometimes make what they hope will be advantageous campaign contributions. (And, of course, after election, they will help the elected candidates pay off their deficits. For example, in 1972, a freshman, Assemblyman Raymond Gonzalez of Bakersfield, attracted considerable attention when he returned to lobbyists checks sent to him after his election. He stated that he had no debts.) All of this leads to conversation and some informal socializing. In addition, lobbyists in recent years have tried a more formal program. "Operation Viewpoint" has been arranged by a bipartisan group of senior legislators and financed by a select group of influential lobbies. In 1966, "Operation Viewpoint" was arranged so that Southern California legislators could tour some of the important sites of Northern California over a week period, and a week later freshmen from the North received a similar tour

of Southern California. The private industries and public institutions sponsoring this program, obviously, were interested in
convincing these newcomers of the "good" intentions of the
sponsoring groups.

And, of course, pre-session legislative socialization begins when
private citizens, community, civic and party leaders begin to contact the legislator-to-be about their problems and needs. Several
freshmen observed that, though not yet being paid as Assembly
members, they were expected by constituents to begin serving the
district as soon as elected. And in trying to render these services,
the freshmen-elect began to play the role of legislators.

Formal Socialization

After the legislature convened in Sacramento, a series of formal
orientation meetings was conducted for the new members.[5] Involved in the orientation process were the Speaker, his staff, members of the Assembly Rules Committee, and the Republican and
Democratic Party caucuses. A considerable part of the orientation
dealt with the "nuts and bolts" aspects of being a legislator. How
bills get drafted, whom to see for particular problems, selecting
secretarial and administrative personnel, and establishing district
offices are examples of the kind of information imparted.[6]

Most of our description of freshman socialization thus far has
focused on the formal, or rather visible and structured, aspects
of early orientation. However, an equally or perhaps more important aspect of the process is the more day-to-day, informal socialization which takes place.

Informal Socialization

As with most legislative bodies, there are considerable opportunities for extensive social contacts in the California Assembly.
During an average week when the legislature is meeting, legislators
from the various parts of the state descend upon Sacramento on
Monday; the first day's session begins normally at 11:00 a.m. They
spend the next several days in Sacramento, leaving for home
usually late Thursday afternoon. This makes most California legislators somewhat analogous to the Tuesday-Thursday group in Con-

gress. A handful of Assembly members, no more than four or five, live within easy commuting distance of Sacramento and drive home evenings. A large number bring their families to Sacramento for the session. However, many legislators (particularly freshmen) are bachelors for the week, and, consequently, a good part of their social life hinges around activities with other legislators.[7] At the end of the day, Sacramento cocktail lounges and restaurants are filled with legislators, lobbyists, reporters, and various state department and agency people, discussing a favorite topic—politics.

Basically, most legislators have a great deal in common, what Duane Lockhard has described as an "in-group" feeling.[8] They have similar schedules: early morning party caucus meeting, office time to handle correspondence, Assembly floor sessions later in the morning, luncheons with visiting constituents, committee hearings in the afternoon, presentation of remarks on behalf of bills before other committees, interviews with radio and television news commentators, as well as college professors and graduate students; and in the evening—banquets, cocktail parties, testimonial dinners, and the like. In this whirl of activity there is a sense of shared problems. Reelection concerns, constituency headaches, work fatigue, family stresses, and party battles are the kinds of problems that all must face. It is not surprising that legislators, usually gregarious and outgoing, should get together frequently to confide in each other, commiserate, and exchange information.

Initial Roles

Compared to congressional freshmen, California Assembly freshmen were exceedingly well treated by their legislative party leaders. They were placed on important committees and were allowed to take an active role in committee from the outset. Their offices and secretarial assistance were also comparable to those of the veteran members.[9] Without exception, veteran members maintained that seniority was not an important factor in the California Assembly.[10] On the other hand, there were some subtle differences between newcomers and veterans. While freshmen could begin to take an immediate role in committee deliberations, the feeling among a number of senior legislators was that they should not say too much on the floor until they had been around for awhile.[11] No freshman was placed on the Ways and Means Committee or elected to the Rules Committee, perhaps the two most critical committees in the Assembly. Senior people tended to have somewhat larger offices, better locations, and more secretaries. As with most legislative bodies, freshmen were considered to be less well-informed than seniors—both substantively and procedurally—and were expected to overcome this liability before taking a full part in the proceedings.

Our interviews with freshmen legislators suggested that socialization in the informal aspects of the legislature comes from two major sources: various individuals in the process and legislative subgroups. During our second interview, we asked: "When you got to Sacramento last January, was there anyone who helped you to learn the ropes, how to do your job? Who were they?" Responses to this question revealed an amazingly rich assortment of legislative socializing sources.

Individuals

The California Assembly newcomers suggested a wide assortment of individuals had helped them find their way through the legislative labyrinth. Several mentioned that committee consultants had been helpful; a few suggested that their secretaries had been of considerable assistance. Some of these secretaries had worked for former Assembly members, and almost all had been part of the capitol milieu for some time. Several Democratic freshmen stated that the Democratic Speaker of the Assembly and several of his staff members provided a great deal of useful information for them. In some cases, freshmen had friends among the senior Assembly members, frequently from adjoining districts, or a senior Senator representing the same constituents.[1][2]

Several newcomers suggested that their seatmates had been of considerable assistance. Physically, California Assembly members are paired in adjoining desks in the Assembly chambers. Generally, an effort is made to put compatible types together as seatmates. Not infrequently, floor sessions—which lawmakers are obligated to attend if they are to receive their per diem—deal with matters of minimal interest—routine technical bills and innocuous resolutions. During these lulls, there are many opportunities to chat with one's seatmate.[13] Customarily, when Assembly members must testify before Senate committees at the same time the Assembly is in session, seatmates are frequently called upon to flick the electronic vote switches of the absent member.[14] The rapport that develops between seatmates helps contribute to the socialization of the new member.

The sources of socialization thus far discussed have been primarily individual; however, a considerable portion of the socialization process comes through a member's association with legislative subgroups operating in the Assembly. Usually, there is no formal course of instruction that these legislative subgroups provide for freshmen, but they do almost imperceptibly, perhaps inadvertently, offer cues for legislative behavior. The new member partially defines his or her role in the Assembly in relation to these groups.

Legislative Subgroups

There are many subgroups operating in the Assembly. Membership in some of these groups comes through invitation, while in others it comes as a matter of course. Demarcation between group members and other legislators is very clear-cut with some groups and very hazy with others. The importance of these groups in legislatures has been stressed by several researchers. At the national level, scholars have suggested that among the functions served by these groups one of the most important is the socializing of congressional freshmen. For example, in discussing this topic, Charles Clapp stated:

> The influence on the views and voting habits of the legislators of participation in these organizations is difficult to measure accurately in concrete terms. But they *are* influential. The opportunities that they provide for mingling informally with colleagues and getting to know them better, for sharing common experiences, for relaxing from the persisting strains of an arduous demanding job, constitute important socializing factors which are difficult to ignore in an assessment of influences on a congressman.[15]

Clapp goes on to say:

They are a means by which to facilitate the indoctrination of freshmen ("The Clubs serve an indoctrination mission. Their members are stray sheep lost in the wilderness who get together to find their way from the House Office Building over to the Capitol.")[16]

Allan Fiellin has also been interested in the role of legislative subgroups in Congress. In a very thoughtful study, Fiellin focused his attention upon the role and functions of one particular legislative subgroup—the Democratic members of the New York State Democratic congressional delegation.[17] He found that this group met on a regular basis, exchanged information about pending legislation, and took positions on a variety of issues.

In sum, these subgroups range from highly structured associations with agendas, regularly scheduled meetings, officers, policy positions, and membership by invitation to, at the other extreme, very tenuous, barely perceptible relationships among numbers of legislators with only the haziest notion of belonging. We have divided the legislative subgroups into two categories: involuntary groups, whose members belong merely because of their membership in the Assembly, and voluntary groups, those whose members must consciously seek to join or be invited to join.

Involuntary Groups

COMMITTEES

A number of legislators suggested that many of their closest friendships in the legislature were gained through committee service. In the California legislature, as in Congress, a legislator's job, and reputation for effectiveness is based to a considerable extent on committee performance. The questions asked witnesses testifying before the committee, suggestions for changing legislation, and ability to carry legislation effectively contribute to one's reputation. Freshman legislators are frequently assigned to the less prestigious committees, though, as we have mentioned, their chances of being placed on important committees are much better than those of congressional freshmen. It is in their membership on a committee that they exercise their judgment and knowledge; and over a period of time, they develop a "committee-sense."

Newcomers are frequently assigned to particular committees

because of their occupational background. Thus, lawyers are often assigned to criminal procedures or judiciary, school administrators and teachers to education, and farmers to agriculture committees. The sort of specialized knowledge focused on specific problems that committee members acquire make them conscious of being part of a special group. For most legislators, the committee becomes "your" committee and an attempt by another legislator to withdraw a bill from *your* committee, or a haphazard presentation by a legislator carrying a piece of legislation before *your* committee is likely to be resented. Probably no other single legislative subgroup is more pervasive or significant in the process of legislative socialization than the committee.

COUNTY AND REGIONAL

For many years, knowledgeable observers of the California legislative process have discerned regional voting blocs in the legislature.[18] Both northern and southern as well as rural and urban voting blocs were reputed to be operating in the legislature. Interviews with California legislators suggested that if the two aforementioned voting splits ever did exist they were no longer perceived to be important factors, though one or two issues might generate this split.[19] However, a few legislators did suggest that there was a special relationship that did develop among members representing a particular county. Traveling to and from Sacramento together, representing similar economic interests, and facing the same regional problems all might help to promote this special rapport.

None of the county delegations which are part of larger regional groupings appears to have anything resembling the structure and organization Fiellin found operating among the Democratic members of the New York delegation in Congress. County and regional groupings did not generally caucus together formally or take public positions, but on matters that did directly affect them (such as the Bay Area Rapid Transit system) special relationships did develop. How closely members from the same county or region work together jointly would depend upon a host of variables including: the nature of the problems affecting the area, the party composition of the group, whether there is a person or persons willing to take the time to organize the group, and the compatibility of the members. It appears that from time to time particular county and regional groups are significant and at other times they may lapse into dormancy depending largely upon the variables suggested above. California legislators are probably less regionally oriented than legislators in other states, since most problems are statewide in nature and neither party is strongly based in any region.[20]

CLASS OF '66

A number of factors encouraged legislators to think of themselves as members of the class of '66. First, there were the northern and southern lobby-sponsored junkets described previously; second, the formal orientation meetings conducted in the state capitol; and third, a number of social affairs designed to acquaint freshman legislators with the Sacramento milieu. All of these activities helped foster friendships and build a sense of unity among the new legislators.

The newcomers all faced the same difficulties. They had to quickly learn a difficult job, gain recognition from their associates, and lay plans for their reelection. The new legislators elected in 1966 were the first beneficiaries of a $10,000 pay hike. Though difficult to prove, it was contended by many Sacramento observers (as well as the freshmen themselves) that the potential pay boost had attracted a group of extremely capable freshmen to the legislature. Freshmen and veterans spoke with considerable pride about the outstanding abilities of the class of '66, and there were frequent references to the number of people who had advanced degrees, or who were lawyers. There seemed to be general agreement among the legislators that the class of '66 was several cuts above the freshman classes of previous sessions.[21] Obviously, the respect that the other legislators had for the freshmen, the sheer number of freshmen, and the freshmen's own pride in their group helped create a sense of class membership. It seems likely that this feeling will diminish as the new members serve a few sessions; however, our discussion with veterans indicates that with most classes there is some lingering influence. Frequently, when we discussed with veteran members the problems they had as freshmen, their answers would be couched in references to the problems members of that particular freshman class had.[22]

PARTY CAUCUS

The development of party caucuses came rather late in the history of the California Assembly (they appeared even later on the Senate side). In the 1967-1968 legislative session, caucuses began to operate for the first time on the Senate side, though a number of senior senators refused to have anything to do with them. On the Assembly side, even though some members had very little "party" loyalty, all members were at least nominally associated with one or the other party caucus.

Party caucuses in the Assembly met on a regular weekly basis to plan strategy, apprise members of pending legislation, and take positions on the issues of the day. Compared to other urban states, cohesion of the Republican and Democratic blocs in the legislature has not been particularly high, and there has been a fair amount of party crossover.[23] Penalties for defying the party caucus position (when one is taken) have generally been subtle forms of ostracism rather than forceful action.

A number of freshmen suggested that the members of the party caucus were very helpful in instructing the new member on the ways of the legislature. Republicans, for example, had the sophomore caucus members discuss with the new GOP members such items as: (1) how they should conduct themselves on the floor and in committee; (2) office procedure; (3) newsletters; (4) parliamentary procedure; (5) press releases; (6) getting legislative counsel opinions; and (7) getting advice on reelection concerns.[24]

Besides this helpful technical instruction in the caucus, freshmen get to know the senior people in their party. A sense of being on the same team appears to develop, and the freshman member of the caucus is told that his or her voting record contributes to the overall record of the party in the legislature. Clearly, the caucus seems to be one of the more important groups in the socialization process.

In addition to the groups listed above, there were a number of other voluntary groups in which freshman consciously sought out membership or were invited to join. We have listed these voluntary groups under three separate headings: dining groups, study and educational groups, and recreation groups.

Voluntary Groups

DINING GROUPS

As mentioned previously, the California legislator is a busy person. Endless rounds of committee hearings, party gatherings, and legislators' meetings make up the day. Because of these time demands, many of the legislative subgroups frequently have their meetings geared around a particular meal, since these are one of the few regular "free" periods in the average legislator's day.

Once every two weeks the "prayer breakfast" group, averaging from ten to fifteen legislators a meeting, gathers early in the morning for worship service and then breakfast. It appears that a camaraderie develops among members of this group. Several freshmen who we interviewed stated that they attended the meetings quite regularly.

One of the more important informal groups was Assemblyman James Bear's Democratic caucus. Formed as a kind of extension of the formal orientation meetings of the first few weeks, "Bear's bunch," as they came to be called, met once a week over coffee and doughnuts. Freshman Democrats who were regulars at these sessions tended to be the younger, more liberal members of the freshman Democratic group. At these meetings, senior legislators and legislative employees presented talks to the freshmen on various aspects of the legislature. Information about pending legislation was exchanged, and a group spirit developed among the legislators in this group. In the second year of the session, this group met only once or twice and during the hectic months before the 1968 primary elections there were no meetings. (Assemblyman Bear was defeated in his reelection bid.) By the second session the freshmen had become "sophomores" and apparently no longer needed this sort of orientation group.

One group of conservative Republican freshmen met with some of their senior conservative colleagues in a number of informal sessions over lunches and dinners in what came to be called by some the "conservative caucus." Prominent in this group were legislators representing Los Angeles, San Diego, and Orange Counties. A somewhat more moderate group of Republican Assembly members, called by some the "young Turk Republicans," also got together over meals. Several of the younger, moderate Republican freshmen could be identified with this group.

Perhaps the most influential dining group in the legislature (at least historically) was the Derby Club, led by one of the ranking senior senators, Senator Randy Collier.[25] Every Tuesday noon certain prominent Assembly members, state Senators, and a few key lobbyists (who picked up the tab) gathered in a special room at Posey's Restaurant a block from the capitol, donned special black derbies, and had lunch together. Freshmen usually were not invited to join this select group, though a few did mention that they had received special invitations to attend a particular luncheon. After the freshman acquires experience, gains the respect of his colleagues, and gets reelected, he may be invited to join this group.

Another lobbyist-financed luncheon gathering was the "moose-milk" group. Though not an exclusive group, since invitations went out to all legislators, there was a subgroup of legislators who regularly attended most gatherings. "Moosemilk" was financed by a broad smattering of lobbyists who pooled their resources and provided a buffet luncheon for legislators every Thursday noon at the Mirador Hotel, a short walk from the capitol. Though legislators suggested that little of political or legislative consequence was discussed at these meetings of legislator and lobbyist, it did provide a place where initial contacts could be made for later appointments in the legislator's office. Obviously, it might be difficult to refuse to hear a lobbyist's views on pending legislation after you had accepted his hospitality at a luncheon.[26]

Formed in reaction to the lobbyist-financed derby and moose-milk groups was a group that came to be called the "mice-milk."[27] This group developed originally out of liberal Democratic Assemblyman John Burton's breakfast group. Assemblyman Burton, along with Assemblyman Willie Brown, a Negro, formed the group as a liberal bloc within the Democratic caucus. The micemilk group members met Tuesdays at noon and brought their lunches in brown bags. By this act, they at least implicitly declared their independence from the lobbyists' largesse. There seems to be some parallel between this group and the Democratic Study Group in the House of Representatives.

STUDY AND EDUCATIONAL GROUPS

Included in the freshman class of '66 were four Black members. Along with two other veteran Black legislators, the "Black caucus" met on an infrequent but regular basis during the session. They discussed policy, considered pending legislation affecting the black community and decided upon possible strategies to employ in seeking their goals.

Evolving from the Black legislators' group and directly overlapping it was the "ghetto discussion group." Organized originally by a white freshman Assemblyman, John Vasconcellos, along with Assemblyman Leon Ralph, a Negro freshman from Watts, members of this group was committed to learning what they could about the problems of the ghetto life. A series of seminars was conducted throughout the session about once every two weeks. Guest speakers were invited to discuss various problems of poverty with the ghetto discussion group. For example, at one meeting, Harry Edwards, San Jose State sociology instructor and one of the leaders of the Black Olympic boycott, appeared. Various aspects of race relations were discussed at this meeting. In all, some fifteen to twenty legislators—primarily the more liberal Democratic members, and particularly many freshmen—attended these informal sessions. Though no formal legislation emanated from the group, several legislators who attended these meetings stated they had gained a new perspective on the problems of the ghetto. It is likely that members attending these sessions were predisposed to support reforms in the ghettos anyway, and their attendance at these seminar discussions probably did not really change this; however, our conversations with legislators associated with this group indicated that those attending these sessions seemed more concerned about the urgency of the situation and more inclined to spend considerable sums alleviating the problems. Members of the ghetto discussion group tended to look upon themselves as providing the impetus for change.

March Fong, a freshman member of the Assembly from Oakland and vice chairman of the Revenue and Taxation Committee, organized a group of freshmen into a series of seminars on fiscal matters. Prominent specialists spoke before "Fong's finance group" in an attempt to equip new members of the committee with knowledge about fiscal matters.

RECREATION GROUPS

Lastly, there were a number of regular and ad hoc groups formed exclusively for relaxation in which freshmen members participated. In addition to the regular poker and gin rummy card groups, there was for the more athletically inclined members (the jocks) who wanted to work out, a group which regularly frequented the Elk's Club gym. Among these recreation groups, the age factor seemed somewhat significant. Older legislators had their regular card groups. Younger legislators had card groups and gym groups.

A Case Study

We have hitherto provided descriptions of several kinds of legislative socialization agencies and a subjective analysis of their effect. In order to better understand the socializing impact of such groups, however, we will now turn to a more empirical analysis of two such agencies—"moosemilk" and "micemilk.[2][8]

Moosemilk has been characterized by capitol observers as a non-ideological, nonpartisan, pro-lobby group. Open to any legislator who wants to attend, it provides ready access and communication contacts between lobbyist and lawmaker. Micemilk, on the other hand, is commonly viewed as ideological (liberal), partisan (Democratic), and anti-lobbyist. While nominally "open" in the sense that any interested legislator could join the group for a weekly lunch, it is to a considerable degree "closed" in that it has a relatively narrow appeal.

Since several freshman members of the class of '66 became active in one or the other group, we have been able to assess the association of interest-group role orientations and group membership over time. If either of these two groups exercised some socializing force, we might reasonably expect freshmen who joined one of them to move toward the group role norm. Specifically, we hypothesised that freshman legislators who join role-oriented informal legislative subgroups will exhibit a change in role toward the group norm.

Interest-group role orientations were determined by use of four agree-disagree scale items originally developed by John Wahlke et al.[2][9] Freshman roles were determined for each of the three periods of time in which we collected interviews. (For a discussion of these items and their use, see Chapter 5 and the Appendices.) First, prior to election; second, after having served one year; and, third, after having been reelected. Group membership was determined during the second and third interviews by asking each respondent:

> When you got to Sacramento did you join any social or other groups? (Formal or informal)
>
> In your off-hours did you tend to spend most of your time with other legislators? What kinds of things would you do?

In answering these questions, our respondents gave us a fairly accurate listing of membership in a number of groups—including moosemilk and micemilk. They not only told us which groups they frequented, but would sometimes casually mention that they often saw Assemblyman X there, or would list two or three of the "regulars."

For the two groups under examination, we found that thirteen freshmen belonged to moosemilk and that nine belonged to micemilk. Eleven were not active in either group. Interestingly enough, four freshmen belonged to both. The pattern of memberships is presented in Figure 3.1.

MOOSEMILK

Contrary to popular assumptions in the state capitol, initial membership in moosemilk did not appear to be strongly associated with a more supportive or sympathetic attitude toward interest groups. The thirteen moosemilk freshmen and the sixteen other nonparticipating freshmen differed little in their interest-group role orientations at the start of their legislative service ($G = .294$). Equally interesting, after a legislator's first term and reelection, the differences in interest-group role orientations between moosemilk freshmen members and other freshmen remained slight ($G = -.248$). In fact, over the two-year period, both moosemilk freshmen and other freshmen became less supportive or sympathetic to interest groups. The only apparent impact that moosemilk had was to slow the trend a slight bit.

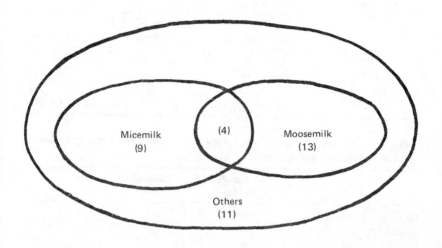

Figure 3.1.

MICEMILK

The micemilk group was, according to some capitol observers, the antithesis of Moosemilk's pro-lobby orientation. Thus, we were surprised to find freshmen micemilk members were no more resister-oriented than were freshmen moosemilk members prior to serving in the legislature. Apparently, the freshmen's initial interest-group role orientation had very little to do with "joining" moosemilk or micemilk.

However, after having served two years in the legislature, the association between group membership and interest-group role orientation was quite substantial (G = −.544; see Table 3.4).

Table 3.1: Freshman Interest Group Role Orientations Prior to Legislative Service, *Moosemilk* and Others

	Moosemilk (N=13)	Others (N=16)	
Resister (< median)	46%	25%	
Median (4.66)	15	25	
Facilitator (> median)	38	50	
			G = .294

Table 3.2: Freshman Interest Group Role Orientations After Legislative Service, *Moosemilk* and Others

	Moosemilk (N=13)	Others (N=16)
Resister (< median)	38%	56%
Median (4.16)	15	6
Facilitator (> median)	46	38
		G = −.248

Table 3.3: Freshman Interest Group Role Orientations Prior to Legislative Service, *Moosemilk* and *Micemilk*

	Moosemilk (N=13)	Micemilk (N=9)
Resister (< median)	45%	45%
Median (4.66)	15	22
Facilitator (> median)	38	33
		G = −.027

Table 3.4: Freshman Interest Group Role Orientations After Legislative Service, *Moosemilk* and *Micemilk*

	Moosemilk (N=13)	Micemilk (N=9)
Resister (< median)	31%	56%
Median (4.00)	8	22
Facilitator (> median)	61	22
		G = −.544

Clearly, there was a meaningful association between micemilk membership and the development of a resister role orientation. Moosemilk had relatively less impact on its members' role orientations—perhaps slowing the trend toward the resister role. Micemilk apparently had a substantial impact on its members' role orientations. Perhaps it only magnified a basic trend discerned among the freshman class as a whole. (A more complete discussion of this role acquisition can be found in Chapter 5.) Nevertheless those who joined micemilk seemed more susceptible to becoming strong resisters. Certainly, micemilk was a more homogeneous group than was moosemilk and, as such, would tend to screen out freshmen who were not substantially similar to its veteran members. We suspect that, in any case, micemilk was a meaningful socializing agent for freshman legislators with regard to interest-group role orientations.

Conclusions

The means by which new legislators are socialized into the legislature are complicated and often not easily discerned. Formal orientation programs conducted by various legislative agents provided a great deal of useful information of a routine, mechanical nature to freshman members. However, the process by which the new legislator is exposed to the informal norm patterns of the legislature, develops institutional pride and, in general, "learns the ropes" is more difficult to assess.

It is clear that there is a host of unwritten rules, traditions, customs, and ways of doing things by which experienced legislators operate and which must be learned and absorbed by the freshmen if the legislature is to run smoothly (this will be extensively examined in Chapter 4). Part of the instruction in these rules comes through individual sources—seatmates, veteran Assembly members from neighboring districts, a particular reporter, a consultant, or a member of the Speaker's staff. However, it was our feeling that an important part of this socializing process, although often inadvertent, comes with the legislator's subgroup associations. Though these groups varied considerably in their exclusiveness, amount of organization, and vagueness of membership, they were similar and important in one regard—as socializers. Freshmen had a wide variety of groups to join, and the associations they chose appeared to have important bearings on their role in the chamber—e.g., the impact of micemilk.

Somewhat unexpectedly, we found that freshman Democrats seemed much more group-oriented than freshman Republicans. Most Democratic freshmen joined several groups, while Republican freshmen either did not need or did not want the close group relationships of the freshman Democrats.

Also, somewhat to our surprise, the groups that seemed to be of greatest importance to the freshmen were of the educational variety such as micemilk, Fong's, ghetto discussion, Bear's bunch, and the conservative caucus.

The friendship and camaraderie which developed among these group members, of course, were not only important in providing cues for freshmen about the unwritten norms, but may well have influenced to a degree their roll-call votes. It is clear that the party caucuses attempted to exert a degree of control over freshmen and senior members of the caucus in regard to their roll-call votes. However, the freshmen's ties with other groups may have also played a significant role in his or her voting record, since most bills in the California Assembly are relatively nonpartisan. For example, the question of when a person's driving rights should be suspended, whether motorcycle drivers should be forced to wear shoes, or the location of a fish hatchery are hardly partisan considerations, but they may generate considerable heat and conflict. It is apparent that on legislation of this type—and a considerable part of the bills introduced are of this nature—friendships and associations which one has developed with other members may be influential in the votes which one casts. In particular, it is crucial on controversial measures in committee. Legislator X, a friend of Legislator Y, might say in committee, "I oppose Y's bill, but I think that all the members should have a chance to record themselves on this measure. I'm going to vote to send this bill out of committee to the floor for third reading.

It should be noted, lastly, that the legislature is not static. With each session there is a new cast of characters, plots, and settings. Groups that were influential and significant during one session may be inconsequential or nonexistent the next session. However, if we are to understand the socialization process in the legislature, how legislators acquire their roles, and how legislators make decisions, we must examine the group structures of the legislature.

NOTES

1. Garland Routt, "Interpersonal Relationships and the Legislative Process," *Annals of the American Academy of Political and Social Science,* Vol. 195 (1938), p. 130.

2. However, it should be noted that the legislator's expenses are considerably greater than average—two homes, frequent trips back "home" to the district, and entertaining constituents are all part of the job.

3. For a useful summarization of factual information dealing with a state legislator's compensation, office and secretarial facilities, and various support agencies, see *American State Legislatures: Their Structure and Procedure* (Chicago: Council of State

Governments, 1967). California either heads the list or is very near the top on virtually every one of the criteria listed. Also see a recent study by the Citizens Conference on State Legislatures, which ranks California's legislature first of all fifty states. See *State Legislatures: An Evaluation of Their Effectiveness* (New York: Praeger, 1971), p. 40.

4. In one instance during the first few weeks of the 1967 session, William Ketchum, a freshman from San Luis Obispo County, brought up a resulution to ratify several charter amendments approved by the people in one of the cities of his district. As the barrage of complicated and contrived questions by senior members of the legislature began, it was cut short by several veteran leaders of the legislature who called for a halt to the game. They suggested that valuable time was being wasted and that a harmful image was being conveyed to the public by this display.

5. At least some of the senior members seemed to resent the fact that this class was provided with so much help. This is how one senior put it: "When I first came here you learned things the hard way. Today they have elaborate orientation programs. They take them by the hand and introduce them to the other legislators, lobbyists, and state bureaucracy. It used to be like the college of twenty years ago—new people had to learn their place. Today new people move right in."

6. For a listing of the forty-four state legislatures having some type of formal orientation program for freshmen see *American State Legislatures,* op. cit., p. 17.

7. There are a number of reasons why many legislators do not bring their families to Sacramento. It is expensive attempting to maintain a second home. There are problems of school transfers for the legislator's children, who are reluctant to move away from their neighborhood and friends. There is a need to maintain contacts back in the home district. Also, having a wife around may be somewhat inhibiting if you want to pursue a political career full time. One legislator touched upon this when he said in an interview with the authors: "In order to be effective here you must put in long hours. You've got to be able to drop down to Jess' [Speaker Unruh] office and have a drink or two at the end of the day. You can't say, 'I've got to go home now; my wife has dinner waiting and I have to give the baby a bath.' " Frankly, we doubt that legislators "drop down" to the Speaker's office, but the point of being able to accept an invitation to do so is still quite valid.

8. Duane Lockhard, "The State Legislator," in *State Legislatures in American Politics,* Alexander Heard, ed. (Englewood Cliffs: Prentice-Hall, 1966). p. 107.

9. Though legislators in the California Assembly were proud of their accommodations, a few of the senior members seemed to resent slightly the kind of offices freshmen were given. One senior stated: "My God, I was just over to X's office. He's got a nicer office than I have. When I came here freshmen got the lousy offices. They had to share desks, secretaries, and had little cubbyholes for offices."

10. Freshmen, who are probably most sensitive to the impact of seniority, consistently rated it as of little significance. It is important to note that neither the speaker, the minority leader, nor the chairmen of the major committees are the most senior members of the Assembly.

11. Veteran legislators rated this as one of the most common mistakes that freshmen were prone to make. This is how one senior legislator described it: "After the primary and general election the freshman is on top of the world. He then must make a rapid transition to being just one of eighty members. Many of the new people try to make names for themselves too quickly. They go off half-cocked or start nit-picking."

Veteran legislators rated the following as some of the other more typical freshmen mistakes: (1) prone to accept bad bills (turkeys) to sponsor; (2) too much coauthoring of legislation; (3) tendency to carry too many bills, and (4) make commitments on votes too early.

12. This is how one veteran described the relationship: "I came here in '63 with the benefit of having X as my senator. I found out what the name of the game was. He gave me many insights. I worked hard meeting people and became acquainted with the guys from both sides. Other freshmen asked me to move legislation on the Senate side. It's easy to go ape in one house, but you need to cultivate the Senate."

13. In several instances, freshmen shared desks and became close friends with their seatmates.

14. Normally, a member voting for his seatmate is never questioned. Recently, though, one legislator objected to the roll-call voting of an absent member. The absent member's seatmate stated that he was testifying before a Senate committee and could not be in the chamber. According to newspaper reports, several unnamed Assembly members stated that the objector had violated one of the unwritten rules of the Assembly with his protestations over the action. See the Sacramento *Bee,* April 18, 1968, p. 5.

15. Charles L. Clapp, *The Congressman* (New York: Doubleday, 1963), p. 41.

16. Ibid., pp. 41-42.

17. Allan Fiellin, "The Functions of Informal Groups in Legislative Institutions," *Journal of Politics,* Vol. 24 (February 1962), pp. 72-91.

18. William Buchanan, *Legislative Partisanship* ("University of California Publications on Political Science," Vol. 13, Berkeley: University of California Press, 1963), pp. 108-122.

19. For a further discussion of this aspect, see Charles G. Bell and Charles M. Price, "Legislative Socialization of Freshman Assemblymen," presented at the 1968 meeting of the Western Political Science Association. Also, see our discussion of regionalism in Chapter 6.

20. Our 1966 interview data suggested that most freshman legislators saw no major difference between district problems and state problems.

21. Though most veteran legislators praised the new people's qualities, a few senior legislators made disparaging remarks about the new crop of freshmen. This is what one veteran said: "They're [freshmen] greedier today. They go to a lobbyist's office. He offers a cigar, and they'll take a handful." Another veteran stated: "I've used the Highway Patrol three or four times since I got here. Some of the freshmen use it like a taxi service."

22. This is how one veteran legislator described his class: "My class was the first one where freshmen began to take an active role. Before my class, freshmen were backbenchers. There were only twenty-seven Republicans when I was first elected. The eleven of us who were freshmen had to carry a tremendous load. We had to learn quickly."

23. Malcolm Jewell, "Party Voting in American State Legislatures," *American Political Science Review,* Vol. 49 (1955), pp. 773-791.

24. However, several freshman Democrats decided their party was losing touch with the youth of the state and that, in turn, the young people of the state, particularly college students, knew little about the complexity of the problems facing California. These freshman leaders organized teams to visit various college campuses and confront students in informal dialogue. In all, about twelve freshman Democrats participated in this effort.

25. Senator Collier was also the head of what came to be dubbed by some members of the Sacramento press corps as "Randy's rat pack." This freeway establishment included the trucking industry, auto clubs, petroleum industry, heavy equipment manufacturers, auto manufacturers, concrete producers, general contractors, the lumber

industry, rock and aggregate producers, and the California Division of Highways. See Bob Simmons, "The Freeway Establishment," *Cry California* (1968), pp. 31-38.

However, as noted in Chapter 1, the derby club was temporarily suspended in January 1975. Proposition 9, sponsored by Common Cause in the 1974 general election, placed severe limits on lobbyist spending. Those limits, combined with uncertainty about other provisions, forced suspension of most lobby-funded entertaining in Sacramento.

26. Our observation of the legislature persuaded us that legislators in California are reasonably accessible. Lobbyists, generally, are able to squeeze in sometime during the day to present their views.

27. A brief description of micemilk may be found in an article by Mary Ellen Leary, "The Democratic New Guard," *The Nation,* March 8, 1971, pp. 302-305.

28. This section is a revision of part of a paper the authors presented at the 1971 meeting of the American Political Science Association. Charles G. Bell and Charles M. Price, "Conflict and Consensus: The Development of Role Orientations and Ideology in Legislative Subgroups."

29. Wahlke et al., op. cit.

Chapter 4

THE RULES OF THE GAME

Introduction

Traditionally, political scientists have concentrated most of their attention upon the formal elements of power in governmental institutions. Legislative research has customarily dealt with topics such as legislative leaders, parliamentary procedure, standing committees, party caucuses, or the intricacies of bill passage.[1] However, another approach to legislative research is now beginning to be explored—the study of informal aspects of the legislative process. For example, legislatures, like all other organized groups, have precise rules which formally define the relationship between members. But, as with other organized groups, legislatures also have certain informal norms, the so-called unwritten rules of the game to which members are supposed to adhere if they want to get along.

These unwritten rules of the game are frequently considered to be as significant as the official by-laws governing groups. Thus, in

AUTHORS' NOTE: This chapter was originally published in somewhat different form in the *Journal of Politics*, XXIII (November 1970), pp. 839-855.

describing the U.S. Senate, Donald R. Matthews writes the following about its unwritten rules, which he describes as *folkways:*

> These folkways, we have suggested, are highly functional to the Senate social system, since they provide motivation for the performance of vital duties and essential modes of behavior which otherwise would go unrewarded. They discourage frequent and lengthy speech-making in a chamber without any other effective limitation on debate, encourage the development of expertness and a division of labor in a group of overworked laymen facing unbelievably complex problems, soften the inevitably personal conflicts of a problem-solving body, and encourage bargaining and cautious use of awesome formal powers. Without these folkways, the Senate could hardly operate with its present organization and rules.[2]

Matthews stresses not only the folkways' significance but also their utility. Several others have also provided substantial insight into the informal rule structure of Congress.[3] However, scholars have just begun to examine the content and impact of the rules of the game at the state level.[4] One could reasonably expect that the "in-group" exclusiveness found in the Senate, or the immense power of certain senior committee chairmen found in the House of Representatives—topics which have been examined by scholars interested in understanding the informal power structures of Congress—might well have their parallels in the state legislatures.

It certainly is attractive to assume that the unwritten rules are at least as important at the state level as at the national level. Professor Duane Lockhard, a former state legislator, suggests this in the following passage:

> Once a session of a state legislature is well under way, an "in-group" feeling begins to develop. Pressure from lobbyists, constituents, party or factional leaders, and the governor induce a fellowship of common cause that transcends party or factional lines. Newcomers, being so numerous, are not frozen out to the extent that freshmen in the United States Congress are, and the membership as a whole relatively soon acquires a sense of shared experiences. The common interest in politics provides a basis for making acquaintances easily; and since politicians tend to be more than normally out-going personalities, there is much more socializing both during and after session hours. The state capitol's hotels are the gathering places for temporary bachelor-legislators who,

being thrown together and not preoccupied by family, spend more time socializing than they would at home. Hotel bars and lobbies, during or after hours, teem with legislators and lobbyists swapping gossip and reminiscing about political exploits.[5]

Not all members, of course, choose to—or perhaps are able to—get along and play by the unwritten rules, though most do. If a member chooses not to abide by the norms of the chamber, he likely will face some form of retribution. This could range from a "cold-shoulder" for minor violations of group norms to the most extreme action, a vote of censure.

Certainly, implicit in the discussions surrounding the rules of the game is the notion that violators will be less effective legislators. Violators will be less likely to be promoted to positions of leadership by their colleagues, and they may have greater difficulty in engineering their bills through the legislative maze. Consequently, we hypothesized that freshmen having the best grasp of the unwritten rules prior to their arrival at the state capitol would be in a better position to move into leadership positions in the shortest time since they would have the greatest understanding of the subtleties of interpersonal relationships in the legislature.

Methods

In this chapter, we are interested in probing into several different aspects of this topic: (1) whether freshmen legislators-to-be (in terms of our model's transitional period) know something about the rules of the game; (2) how extensive their knowledge of this subject is; (3) whether there are some kinds of pre-legislative experience associated with knowledge about the rules of the game; (4) whether greater knowledge of the rules results in some legislators being more effective than others; and (5) finally, whether greater knowledge of the rules results in more rapid advancement into positions of influence within the legislature.

In order to establish the formal framework for pursuing these questions, we posited the following hypotheses concerning the rules of the game.

Our major hypothesis was that legislators-to-be with considerable understanding and feeling for the unwritten rules and informal customs of the assembly would be more likely to rise to positions of influence within the Assembly during their first years in the legislature than would their less prepared colleagues.

Our minor hypotheses were:

(1) Legislators-to-be with prior legislative experience (city council, board of supervisors, or school board) would be more knowledgeable of the rules of the game than would those with no .such prior experience;

(2) education would be positively associated with knowledge of the rules of the game;

(3) political experience in campaigns or as a member of a political club would be positively associated with knowledge of the rules of the game; and

(4) activity with community/civic organizations would be positively associated with knowledge of the rules of the game.

Findings

INITIAL KNOWLEDGE

In order to find out whether legislators-to-be understood something about the unwritten rules, we asked the following question:

We have been told that the Assembly, like most other groups, has its own unofficial rules, the rules of the game, things members should do and should not do if they want the respect and cooperation of other members. What are some of the rules of the game that you expect to find in the Assembly?[6]

A substantial majority of the respondents had heard about the rules of the game and could explain to some extent the nature of these norms. Of the thirty-one interviewees, twenty-three (74%) were able to specifically suggest what some of the rules of the game were. To facilitate analysis, the unwritten rules that the legislative aspirants perceived to be operating in the assembly were classified under three headings: (1) *individual and interpersonal*, the rules of general conduct operating in the legislature; (2) *legislative*, the "dos and don'ts" of the legislative process; and (3) *party*, the relationship between party leaders and a member of the party caucus. A listing of the rules of the game suggested by re-

Table 4.1: Rules Suggested Prior to Legislative Experience

Individual and Interpersonal	Respondents Citing Specific Rules	Legislative	Respondents Citing Specific Rules
1. treat all with courtesy and respect	(6)	1. rely on legislative leaders	(2)
2. keep your word—don't double cross	(6)	2. do your homework	(1)
3. don't personally attack other members	(5)	3. know what you're talking about	(1)
4. seniority affects freshmen	(3)	4. loyalty to Speaker	(1)
5. may differ publicly, but privately you're friends	(2)	5. personal feelings should not influence your voting	(1)
6. a great deal of camaraderie	(1)	6. informal rules more important than formal legislative ones	(1)
7. be on the job—no goofing off	(1)		
8. keep your mouth shut	(1)	7. member does not attack another's bill in committee	(1)
9. be honest	(1)	8. informal clubs	(1)
10. help one another	(1)	9. must horse-trade for votes	(1)
11. go along	(1)	10. don't pin a member on a vote	(1)
12. don't move too fast	(1)	11. avoid a roll call if it will be painful to others	(1)
13. be open and frank	(1)		
14. overlook differences	(1)		
15. don't carry grudges	(1)		
16. socialize together	(1)		
17. trust fellow members	(1)	*Party*	
18. use discretion	(1)	1. in caucus say what you damn please—but not on the floor	(1)
19. don't catch members by surprise	(1)	2. people in party must get along	(1)
20. don't overdo publicity	(1)	3. a good Democrat delivers	(1)

spondents, and a tabulation of the number of times each was cited, is contained in Table 4.1.

Though the three classificatory headings may be somewhat general and arbitrary, several conclusions can be suggested.[7] It is clear that the rules most frequently cited by the legislative aspirants were primarily of the individual and interpersonal variety. John Wahlke and his colleagues found a similar emphasis on the interpersonal rules among California legislators in the late 1950s. They suggest that this may be in part due to the individualistic tradition and nonpartisan atmosphere in California politics.[8] Since our data are drawn from pre-legislative interviews, the larger political/cultural milieu appears to be the dominant factor.

The norms described are essentially the unwritten rules customary to most groups. For example, the two rules most frequently cited "treat all with courtesy and respect" and "keep your word—don't double cross" indicate clearly an awareness by most freshmen of the need to get along. Yet awhile a substantial variety of individual and interpersonal rules were suggested, several of them repeatedly, only a handful of legislative or party rules were mentioned by the respondents. Knowledge in the latter two areas appears to come with legislative service.[9]

It is interesting to note that among the twenty-three respondents having some knowledge of the rules, none suggested that he or she would not try to accommodate him- or herself to these norms. In fact, none of the legislative aspirants expressed the slightest disapproval of the rules. Even when rules were suggested which were clearly not idealistic, such as "must horse-trade for votes," the legislative aspirant described the rules objectively rather than in a negative fashion. One could speculate that future legislative mavericks (those members who defy institutional norms) might come from the ranks of the eight (26%) who knew nothing about the rules and who might be startled by what was expected of them. On the other hand, because a member is able to suggest what the rules of the game are does not guarantee in all cases that the member will abide by them.

ROOTS OF RULE SOPHISTICATION

As might be expected, the thirty-one legislative aspirants' knowledge ranged along a continuum from essentially complete ignorance to relatively sophisticated descriptions of the rules of the game. Although there were no hard-and-fast lines separating the respondents along this continuum, it was clear that some respondents were able to explain in fairly sophisticated terms what rules they expected to find while others were simply unable to respond to this question.[10] Three questions in particular measured the respondent's understanding of the informal norms of the assembly. First, the question already referred to dealing with a description of the rules of the game. Second, in a follow-up question, the respondents were asked what would happen if the rules of the game were violated.[11] Third, respondents were asked, "There have been rumors that the present Speaker may have opposition in his bid for reelection next January. What effect would it have on your activities as an Assemblyman if you voted for the losing candidate?"[1][2] Aspirants' responses to each of these questions were then evaluated on a five-point scale which ran something like this:

4 highly sophisticated response to question, respondent cites a number of different examples;

3 knowledgeable response to question, though lacking some of the subtle nuances of the above—fewer examples, less expansive;

2 brief, somewhat inadequate response to question, cites only one example—answer vague and general;

1 attempts answer but fails to indicate that he understands what is asked; and

0 fails to respond or says he does not know.

Based upon the scope and sophistication of their answer, respondents were given a rating for each of the three questions. Ratings from each of the three questions were then averaged, and an overall Rule Sophistication Score was tabulated.[13] Scores ranged from a high of 3.6 to a low of 0.7. In order to facilitate analysis of these data, the upper half of the group of aspirants (scores of 2.8 or higher) were classified as "sophisticated," and the lower half (2.7 and under) were classified as "naive." Admittedly, the dividing line separating the sophisticated from the naive is arbitrary; it was our feeling, however, that those near the 3.0 score and above indicated in a reasonably consistent fashion that they were aware of the content and meaning of the unwritten rules of the legislature. Members in the lower half quite clearly were less knowledgeable about the norms they would find operating in the Assembly.[14]

What background features distinguished the sophisticated from the naive? Did the sophisticated have a better education, more social contacts, and more extensive political experience? Did the sophisticated tend to have any particular educational or occupational background? Lastly, were there any discernible differences in role orientations between the sophisticated and the less aware?

Political Background. It is clear from the data in Table 4.2 that party affiliation and, to an even greater extent, ideology correlate with initial rule sophistication. Democrats and liberals (frequently coterminous) were more likely to be knowledgeable about the

Table 4.2: Political, Professional, Educational and Community Background
Correlates to Rule Sophistication

Variable:[b]	Correlation to Rule Sophistication Score[a]
Party affiliation (Democrat)	.483*
Ideology (Liberal)	.727*
Been active in other campaigns (Yes)	.242
Active club member before running (Yes)	−.407*
Held appointive office before running (Yes)	.086
Had run for office previously (Yes)	.366*
Had held elective office before running (Yes)	.098
Had held party position before running (Yes)	.079
College major (Social science or humanities)[c]	.156
Occupation (Lawyer)[c]	.238
Active in social or community groups (Five or more)[d]	.232
Officer in social or community groups (Yes)	.029

*Correlation statistically significant at $\leqslant$.05. However, as we interviewed thirty-one out of thirty-three freshmen, tests for statistical siginficance appear meaningless.
a. Biserial correlation technique, see Robert H. Koenker, **Simplified Statistics** (Illinois: McKnight and McKnight, 1961), p. 140.
b. Each variable has been dichotomized, the value in parenthesis is associated with rule sophistication as indicated by the sign. Insertion of the alternative value ("Republican," "Conservative," "No," etc.) would reverse the sign of the reported correlation.
c. The alternative is "Other."
d. The alternative of the dichotomous variable is "four or less.'

rules prior to their assumption of office than were Republicans and conservatives (also frequently coterminous). None of the other political activity factors appeared to correlate in a very substantial way with sophistication. However, there is some suggestion that the naive freshmen had previously been less politically active than the sophisticated had been.

Interestingly, one aspect of political activity appears to correlate negatively with sophistication. Respondents active in political clubs tended to be more naive than those who had not been active. Exactly why the positive association between political participation and rule sophistication should be reversed here is not clear. It ·is possible that the less aware may have exaggerated the extent of their participation, feeling that they "ought" to have been more active than they were. On the other hand, the sophisticated may have unduly minimized the time spent in club activities, particularly in contrast to their campaign efforts. Nevertheless, even with this one item to the contrary, it sppears that the sophisticated tended to have been more active politically than the naive prior to their assuming legislative office.

Educational and Occupational Background. In most respects, the freshman class was not typical of the state's adult population. There was the usual overwhelming male predominance among the freshmen (only two of the newly elected members were women), and in terms of education and socioeconomic background, new members were far from typical. Each of the legislative aspirants had completed at least some college work; only four were not college graduates. Over a third of the new members were attorneys, and a number of others had completed some postgraduate work. Since all of the aspirants had completed at least some college work, there was little point in comparing levels of education with levels of sophistication.

One point of interest, however, in this regard was whether the respondents' college major was related to the candidate's sophistication score. We conjectured that people majoring in the social sciences and humanities would be more likely to be sophisticated than those from other disciplines. In addition, it was hypothesized that there would be a positive correlation between attorneys and the sophisticated. The give and take of the courtroom, its formalized ritual and informal rules, and the constant search for compromise would seem to provide an excellent grounding in the rules of the game for freshmen legislators. One respondent, in fact, referred to the close parallel between courtroom and legislature in his response to the rules of the game question. He stated:

> The rules of the game in the legislature are like those operating in the courtroom. It's like lawyers fighting and arguing in court, and then afterwards getting together and having a drink.

However, the correlations between sophistication and both occupation and type of education were quite low. Type of college major clearly did not correlate appreciably with level of sophistication. And, although there does appear to be some slight evidence to suggest that lawyers tended to have a higher sophistication score, the correlation was hardly substantial.

Social-Community Involvement. It was further hypothesized that respondents having extensive community club memberships, and those who had participated in a variety of community activities, would have a greater feeling for rules of the game than those

Table 4.3: Legislative Roles and Rule Sophistication[a]

	r_{bis}[b]
Representative Role	
1. The job of an Assemblyman is to work for what his constituents want even though this may not always agree with his personal view.	.000
2. An Assemblyman can decide how to vote on most issues by asking himself if the proposed law is morally right.	−.602*
3. I will seldom have to sound out my constituents because I think so much like them that I know how to react to almost any proposal.	−.217
4. With his better sources of information, an Assemblyman should vote as he thinks best, even when his constituents disagree.	.630*
Interest Group Role	
5. Under our form of government every individual should take an interest in government directly not through interest group organizations.	.256
6. I expect interest groups or their agents will give me valuable help in lining up support for my bills.	.012
7. I expect to get valuable help in drafting bills or amendments from interest groups or their agents.	−.486*
8. Interest groups have entirely too much influence in the California Legislature today.	.399*
Party Role	
9. The best interests of the people would be better served if Assemblymen were elected without party labels.	−.332
10. If a bill is important for his party's record, an Assemblyman should vote with his party even if it costs him some support in his district.	−.220
11. It's just as important to be on guard against ideas put out by people of one's own party as against ideas put out by people of the opposite party.	−.312
12. Under our form of government every individual should take an interest in government directly, not through a political party.	−.134
Professional Role	
13. The legislature is a full-time job.	.266
14. The salaries of Assemblymen ought to be substantially increased.	.016
15. The legislature should meet most of the year like Congress.	.301
16. More staff and research facilities should be available to the Assembly.	.403*

*Statistically significant at $p \leqslant .05$.
a. Ordinarily, these items would have been combined into role scores for the purposes of analysis. However, after considerable use and analysis of these items, we have reached the conclusion that they are sometimes better used as single items, e.g., see the correlations for items number 2 and 4.
b. All biserials have been calculated so that a plus sign means the variable is positively associated with "Sophistication." Note: Even though a few of the variables are truly dichotomous, the biserial has been used rather than the point biserial. This is in order to maintain comparability of correlation figures.

who were not as active in community groups. However, the correlations in Table 4.2 indicate that this was not the case. Obviously, our hypothesis must be rejected; the number of community groups in which respondents belonged and the level of involvement in community activities failed to associate in any substantial way with sophistication.

Roles. Up to now we have considered the differences in the general backgrounds of the sophisticated and the naive and have come to certain conclusions about the type of person each was. In order to add a further dimension to this analysis, a series of agree-disagree statements was asked freshmen to determine their attitudes about legislative roles.[15] (These roles are extensively discussed in Chapter 5.) Each freshman was asked how strongly he or she agreed or disagreed with each of the statements listed in Table 4.3. The strength of his attitude was measured by using a nine-point scale, ranging from −4 for strongly disagree to a +4 for strongly agree.

For most of the role statements, there was no substantial difference between the attitudes of the sophisticated and those of the naive. However, a few of the role item correlations revealed substantial differences. The sophisticated agreed more emphatically that the legislature should meet most of the year, and that there was a need for more staff. The direction of these attitudes is consistent also on the statement that the legislature is a full-time job. Rather surprisingly, there was little difference between the sophisticated and the naive in responses to raising salaries. But, on the whole, the sophisticated tended to have a more professionalized view of the legislature.

Statements dealing with interest groups produced two moderately high correlations. Unexpectedly, the sophisticated seemed to be more resister than facilitator. In particular, the sophisticated were not disposed to receiving aid from interest groups in drafting legislation, and they seemed much more concerned with the problem of group influence in the legislature.[16]

Two party statements also produced moderately low correlations with the sophisticated taking a somewhat more partisan position than the naive. The naive were more disposed to having Assembly members elected without party labels and were more likely to feel that a legislator had to be on guard against ideas put out by people of one's own party as well as those of the other party.

EFFECTS OF RULE SOPHISTICATION

Effectiveness. Our prime interest in this chapter was in discerning the relationship between the Assembly aspirant's understanding of the rules of the game and his subsequent legislative effectiveness. The few social scientists who have examined the phenomenon have *suggested* that knowledge about the rules is associated with legislative effectiveness. The California Assembly afforded an excellent setting in which to explore this question. Unlike Congress and some state legislatures, seniority in the lower house of California has never been a particularly important factor. Freshman members, depending upon their abilities and political skills, have traditionally been able to play important roles in the Assembly from the outset of their careers. And, often enough, second- and third-term Assembly members became committee chairmen.

Though, obviously, legislative effectiveness is a nebulous concept, it is used frequently by state capitol reporters, political scientists, and legislators themselves. Essentially, it would seem, an effective legislator introduces and carries some of the significant legislation of a particular session, plays an important role in his committees, skillfully maneuvers his bills through the legislature, gets elected or selected to key legislative positions, defeats legislation he opposes, and in general achieves his legislative goals. In order to assess the effectiveness of the individual members of the freshmen class, we asked each of them after one year's service and again in the early part of their second term, which members of their class they considered the most effective. (For comparative purposes, we asked this same question of most of the senior members as well.) We did not define "effective" for our respondents. Each freshman was given an "effectiveness score" equal to the number of times he was nominated by his peers as "effective." We have not used the "effective" nominations obtained during the third interview (1969) as the appointment of several freshmen to committee chairmanships at the beginning of the 1969 session altered the meaning of the term.

Interestingly, there was no significant association between sophistication and effectiveness. Calculation of a rank correlation between the two variables produced a negligible association of .176. And, while we found a moderately strong association between party and sophistication (.483, see Table 4.1), we found only a weak association between party and effectiveness of .215.[17] Clearly, then, neither party nor initial sophistication about the rules of the game meant much in peer perception of effectiveness.

Rapid Promotion. The 1968 elections in California tipped the state Assembly into Republican hands for the first time in a decade. A new speaker, Robert Monagan, Republican from Tracy, replaced Democrat Jess Unruh and, along with this shift in power, committee chairmanships and committee assignments were also changed. While seniority is a factor in the Speaker's decision to place people on committees and to select committee chairmen, it has been by no means either the most important or only factor.[18] Other factors such as intelligence, knowledge of the subject field, occupational background, ties to the Speaker, party, and requests of individual members have been, in most cases, equally or more important.

But, until recently, political party was perhaps the least crucial of these factors.[19] Though party has sometimes been important in the past, members of the minority party always received some committee chairmanships. In the last few years, however, party has become an increasingly important factor. As a result, the Republican Speaker designated only *one* Democrat from the class of '66 to chair a committee. (Our freshmen were at this point sophomores, having been reelected in 1968.) Thus, our analysis of the relationship between rule sophistication and rapid advancement to position of influence is focused on class of '66 Republicans only. Two categories were established: the successful, and the unsuccessful.

The successful were those Republicans of the class of '66 who were appointed committee chairmen or who were placed on either the Rules Committee or the Ways and Means Committee; the unsuccessful were Republican freshmen who did not attain these positions.[20] Calculation of the biserial correlation between rule sophistication and success produced a meaningless .037. Thus, it appears that having a solid understanding of the rules of the game *prior* to service in the legislature does nothing to enhance the legislator's subsequent ability to move ahead in the chamber.

Summary

While a substantial majority of Assembly aspirants had some knowledge of the rules, the differences in knowledge were wide enough to permit a crude ranking and assignment of "sophistication scores." Most of the rules cited by freshmen Assemblymen prior to legislative service were of the standard interpersonal type: be courteous, honest, reliable, etc. Only a few of the legislators-to-be cited some specifically legislative or party rules.

Initial rule sophistication was associated with both political party and ideology, with Democrats and liberals tending to be more sophisticated than Republicans or conservatives. The sophisticated appear to have been somewhat more active politically than the unsophisticated, though the pattern was neither as strong nor as consistent as expected. Surprisingly, education, occupation, and community activity were not associated with rule sophistication.

Comparing rule sophistication to a number of legislative role items produced only a few substantial associations. The strongest association appeared to be with representative-style role orientation; the sophisticated strongly disagreed with the statement that they could decide how to vote on most issues by asking themselves what was morally right, which suggests a delegate role. Conversely, and just as strongly, they agreed that a legislator, with his better sources of information should vote as he thinks best, which suggests the trustee role. Correlations to the other role items were not as strong but more clear-cut, suggesting that the sophisticated tend to play the partisan party role, the resister interest-group role, and the professional legislator role.

Perhaps the most interesting finding was that there was no meaningful association between initial rule sophistication and subsequent legislative effectiveness nor with eventual important committee assignments. There was no indication in the sophistication scores, which we developed from our pre-legislative service interviews, that sophistication was associated with subsequent appointment as committee chairmen or to a prestigious Assembly committee.

These results essentially present us with one of two choices. First, it is possible that the rules of the game as they are understood by political scientists are not very important. Or, second, the initial gross disparity between legislative aspirants was substantially reduced during legislative service. Of the two alternatives, we tend to support the second. Data gathered in subsequent interviews with the same legislators indicate that initial differences in interpersonal rule sophistication between freshmen were substantially reduced. In fact, we were unable to make any valid scoring of rule sophistication based on our subsequent interviews with the class of '66.

In addition, the nature of the rules cited in the subsequent interviews was substantially different. A whole host of "in-house" norms were cited after legislative experience. Rules pertaining to committee decorum and the management of bills were frequently cited in the first interview. This kind of knowledge appears to be as important in getting ahead in the legislature as are the more general interpersonal rules. Our findings strongly suggest a substantial legislative socializing of the rules of the game. What the freshman knew of the rules before his legislative career appears not to be very important. What he learned during the first term appears to have been very important.

NOTES

1. The literature dealing with these topics is voluminous. One of the best current examples of a study dealing with the formal and informal rule structures in Congress is by Lewis A. Froman, Jr., *The Congressional Process* (Boston: Little, Brown, 1967).

2. Donald R. Matthews, *U.S. Senators and Their World* (New York: Vintage Books, Division of Random House, 1960), p. 92.

3. In addition to Matthews' work, David Trumen, *The Governmental Process* (New York: Alfred A. Knopf, 1951), pp. 343-345, emphasizes the critical importance of these unwritten rules in Congress. Charles Clapp discusses these informal norms in his *The Congressman* (Garden City, N.Y.: Doubleday, Anchor, 1963). Ralph Huitt describes some of the problems a freshman faces in adapting to the informal norms of the Senate in "The Outsider in the Senate: An Alternative Role," *American Political Science Review* LV (September 1961), pp. 566-576. Malcolm Jewell and Samuel C. Patterson discuss this topic at some length at both the Congressional and state levels in *The Legislative Process in the United States* (New York: Random House, 1966). Allan Kornberg, in a very useful article, analyzes these rules in the Canadian House of Commons in his "The Rules of the Game in Legislative Politics: A Comparative Study," *Journal of Politics* XXVI (May 1964), pp. 358-380.

4. Three of the most important studies dealing with rules of the game at the state level are: John C. Wahlke et al., *The Legislative System* (New York: John Wiley, 1962); James D. Barber, *The Lawmaker: Recruitment and Adaptation to Legislative Life* (New Haven, Conn.: Yale University Press, 1965); and Samuel C. Patterson, "The Role of the Deviant in the State Legislative System: The Wisconsin Assembly," *Western Political Quarterly* XIV (June 1961), pp. 460-472.

5. Duane Lockhard, "The State Legislator," in *State Legislatures in American Politics*, Alexander Heard, ed. (Englewood Cliffs, N.J.: Prentice-Hall, 1966), p. 107.

6. This question, altered slightly, was used originally by Wahlke et al., op. cit., p. 143.

7. For example, it was difficult to decide whether separate listings should be made for such responses as "be honest" and "be open and frank" or whether these mean essentially the same thing. The four-state study by Wahlke and his group used six categories: rules primarily to promote group cohesion and solidarity; rules which primarily promote predictability of legislative behavior; rules which primarily channel and restrain conflict; rules which primarily expedite legislative business; rules which serve primarily to give tactical advantages to individual members, and desirable personal qualities cited as rules. Wahlke et al., op. cit., pp. 160-161.

8. Wahlke et al., Ibid., p. 150.

9. This conclusion is supported by other data reported in Ronald Hedlund, "Legislative Socialization and Role Orientations," The Laboratory for Political Research, University of Iowa, Report 11, October 1967, and also, Charles G. Bell and Charles M. Price, "Pre-Legislative Sources of Legislator's Role Orientations," presented at the 1969 annual meeting of the American Political Science Association.

10. Four of the new members elected to the legislature had spent a considerable amount of time in Sacramento prior to their election serving in various staff positions. These four in terms of legislative service were freshmen; in terms of legislative experience in Sacramento, they were veterans.

11. Some of the sanctions suggested were: (1) limiting your effectiveness; (2) difficulty getting your bills through; (3) assigned to less prestigious committees; (4) no junkets; (5) ostracism; (6) no social acceptance, and (7) no interim committee assignments.

12. California's Assembly Speaker is extremely influential. His power derives to a considerable extent from his ability to designate committee chairmen and committee members and assign bills to committee. Being in the good graces of the Speaker meant assignment to the right committee, help for your bills, and the chance to occupy some of the choicer assembly office suites. Though there was no "right" answer to this question on the Speaker, we were interested in knowing if the respondents had some feeling for the consequences of the vote for Speaker.

13. These three items correlate satisfactorily with the sum of all three by use of gamma. Item 1 with a .71, Item 2 with a .66, and Item 3 with a .83.

14. There are a number of problems one faces in attempting to evaluate the level of sophistication a respondent registers through examining his response to a series of questions. Some people are simply more expansive than others, and thus provide "better" interviews. If the interviewee had other appointments, had other things on his mind, or simply had had a bad day, his answers to the questions might be rather curt and abrupt. Some members might have recognized a particular rule as operating but were unable to recall it when asked. Nevertheless, these limitations notwithstanding, we believe the responses of the thirty-one aspirants to the three questions provide us with a rough, but reasonably accurate, gauge of a candidate's sophistication.

15. Many of these role items were originally developed by Wahlke et al., op. cit., pp. 502-503.

16. This latter association may be explained by the fact that interest groups are generally considered to be quite strong in California. See Wahlke et al., op. cit., pp. 313-323.

17. Biserial technique.

18. Richard Brandsma and Al Sokolow found that the three most important Assembly committees had somewhat higher tenure averages than most of the other Assembly committees. The figures were: Ways and Means members' average tenure, 9.94 years; Rules, 4.0; and Revenue and Taxation, 6.14. Richard W. Brandsma and Alvin D. Sokolow, "Strategy and Culture in Legislative Committee Assignments: California in 1967," presented at the Western Political Science Association Meeting, Seattle, Washington, March 21-23, 1968, p. 23.

For a comprehensive examination of the committee system in the California Legislature see Sokolow's chapter "The Member and the Standing Committee," in *The Legislative Process in California,* by Joel M. Fisher, Charles M. Price, and Charles G. Bell, (Washington, D.C.: American Political Science Association, 1973).

19. See William Buchanan, *Legislative Partisanship* (Berkeley: University of California Press, 1963).

20. The Assembly Rules Committee members are selected by election in the majority and minority party caucuses. The chairman of this committee is selected by the Speaker like all other committee chairmen.

Chapter 5

THE DEVELOPMENT OF LEGISLATORS'
ROLE ORIENTATIONS

Introduction

Role theory or, in application, role analysis has become increasingly significant in the social sciences in recent years.[1] The term "role" first came into general usage as a result of the work by anthropologist Ralph Lintin in the mid-1930s; however, others, such as C. H. Cooley and J. L. Moreno must also be given substantial credit for their early contributions.[2] There are many definitions of role, but the one offered by Eugene L. and Ruth E. Hartley seems particularly useful. According to the Hartleys, role is essentially the total pattern of expectations having to do with norms, tasks, attitudes, values, and reciprocal relationships associated with an individual's position within a system.[3] Role, Neal Gross and associates suggest, has three elements: social location,

AUTHORS' NOTE: Some parts of this chapter were presented in a paper at the 1969 annual meeting of the American Political Science Association. A small part of it was published as "Pre-Legislative Sources of Representational Roles," *Midwest Journal of Political Science,* XIII (May 1969), pp. 254-270.

behavior, and expectations.[4] It is important, moreover, to distinguish between status or position and role. Linton points out: "A status, as distinct from the individual who may occupy it, is simply a collection of rights and duties. . . . A *Role* represents the dynamic aspect of status."[5] This difference becomes obvious when one considers the fact that an individual occupying the position of President of the United States may play *several* different roles—chief of state, commander-in-chief, chief executive, chief legislator, leader of his party, or leader of his nation. Thus, the term "role" includes some form of acting, behaving, or the holding of an attitude. In this chapter, we shall explore the acquisition by California legislators of certain role orientations and role expectations both from their legislative experience and from pre-legislative experience.

Since legislators (like the President or the governor) play a number of different roles, this analysis will, hopefully, give us a realistic model of the legislator as an active, institutionalized human being. As John C. Wahlke points out in *The Legislative System:* "The chief utility of the role-theory model of the legislative actor is that, unlike other models, it pinpoints those aspects of legislators' behavior which make the legislature an institution."[6] Not surprisingly, many political scientists have become interested in studying legislative roles and have done considerable research in this general area.[7]

However, not all political scientists are enthusiastic about role analysis. Wayne Francis has questioned whether or not role by itself is a meaningful concept, suggesting that a concept which is so broad must surely have some deficiencies.[8] Francis contends that role does not explain behavior and that little has been done to demonstrate any relationship between legislative role and roll call votes (as one type of legislative behavior).[9] Another criticism of role is that some of the role typologies are inadequate. For example, Kenneth Janda has suggested that the politico role is not a role. Legislators who "play" this role are, in fact, not playing any representational role at all.[10]

In spite of the reservations expressed by Janda, Francis, and others, role seems to us to be a very promising conceptual framework within which to examine and explain legislative behavior. It allows the researcher to relate one legislator to other legislators, to lobbyists, to bureaucrats, to constituents, and to a whole host of other actors in the legislative system. In this chapter, we will examine the development of legislative role orientations.

In their seminal study of four state legislatures, Wahlke and associates developed and intensively examined a number of different legislative role typologies. In fact, with the exception of the representative role, the other roles posited were essentially original work. In this chapter, we shall consider three role typologies: representational, interest group and party.[11]

"Representative role" is categorized on a trustee-politico-delegate continuum.[12] A legislator with a trustee viewpoint determines, on the basis of one's own judgement and values, how he or she should vote in the legislature. A delegate, on the other hand, votes the way one perceives constituents to want him or her to vote. A politico generally follows a middle course, acting sometimes as a trustee and sometimes as a delegate. The "interest group role" is categorized on a resister-neutral-facilitator continuum. A resister legislator is hostile toward interest groups; a facilitator legislator is friendly and receptive to interest groups, while a neutral legislator has no strong attitude toward interest groups. The "party role" is categorized on a partisan-nonpartisan-anti-partisan continuum. A partisan legislator is inclined to view the actions of party leaders and caucus in a favorable light; the antipartisan is suspicious and hostile toward party activity in the legislature, while the nonpartisan is neither friendly nor hostile to parties. (Wahlke et al., op. cit., define the party role continuum as "party man" or as "independent, maverick or nonpartisan," p. 359.) Interestingly, while the polar roles (i.e., trustee or delegate, facilitator or resister, and partisan or antipartisan) have received considerable attention, the middle roles of politico, neutral and nonpartisan have not been examined in much depth.

Moreover, to date, much more has been done to describe and define legislative roles than to explain why legislators adopt one rather than another. It is our intention in this chapter to get at some of the roots of political roles—in other words, role socialization.

Traditionally, studies of role behavior in legislatures have focused upon incumbent representatives. But if we are to understand the meaning and process of role acquisition by the legislator, it is vital to assess these roles prior to the legislator's election in the pre-paratory legislative socialization phase. Only in this way can we achieve any valid measure of the relative impact of pre-legislative life. And only by doing this can we assess the impact of legislative service upon these roles in the specific socialization phase. Certainly, it cannot be assumed that legislative roles are derived solely from legislative experiences. As Wahlke points out:

> Legislators do not begin to acquire and form their legislative role concepts and orientations only at the official dawn of their legislative careers. . . . We can, therefore, conceive that each legislator-to-be possesses some sort of "role potential."[13]

Thus, our first objective in this chapter is to determine the initial role orientations of legislators-to-be and to consider some of the pre-legislative factors which may have given rise to them. Following that, we shall attempt to assess the impact of legislative experience upon these roles and, finally, we shall examine the development of legislative role systems—the way in which roles are related to each other.

Our data are drawn from three separate interviews with the freshman legislators and a separate interview with the veterans. Each of the respondents was given the same role scale items at each interview.

Method

In each of the interviews, respondents were given the same nine role scale items and asked to indicate how strongly they agreed or disagreed with each item. (In fact, four items per role were used, but one item per role failed to meet item analysis tests.) This is the scale we used.

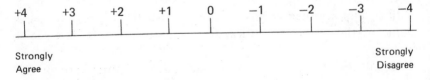

+4   +3   +2   +1   0   −1   −2   −3   −4

Strongly   Strongly
Agree   Disagree

The role items used were:

REPRESENTATIVE ROLE ITEMS

(1) The job of an assemblyman is to work for what his constituents want even though this may not always agree with his personal view.

(2) I will seldom have to sound out my constituents because I think so much like them that I know how to react to almost any proposal.

(3) With his better sources of information, an assemblyman should vote as he thinks best even when his constituents disagree.

INTEREST-GROUP ROLE ITEMS

(4) Under our form of government, every individual should take an interest in government directly, not through interest group organizations.

(5) Interest groups or their agents will give me valuable help in lining up support for my bills.

(6) Interest groups have entirely too much influence in the California Legislature today.

PARTY ROLE ITEMS

(7) The best interests of the people would be better served if assemblymen were elected without party labels.

(8) It's just as important to be on guard against ideas put out by people of one's own party as against ideas put out by people in the opposite party.

(9) Under our form of government, every individual should take an interest in government directly, not through a political party.

These nine role items were scattered through a larger battery of sixteen items. Several of the items were reversed to reduce set response. Each legislator's role score, ranging from 0.00 to 8.00, is the sum of three role item scores divided by three.

The Development of Legislative Roles

Initial Role Orientations. Prior to legislative service, the California legislator-to-be tended to take middle role positions. As Table 5.1 illustrates, relatively few took polar role positions prior to legislative service. Sixty-two percent took the politico (representational) role, sixty-five percent took the neutral (interest-group)

Table 5.1: Pre-Legislative Role Orientations

Representative Role		Party Role		Interest Group Role	
Trustee	10%	Partisan	24%	Resister	7%
Politico	62	Nonpartisan	69	Neutral	65
Delegate	28	Antipartisan	7	Facilitator	28

role, and sixty-nine percent took the nonpartisan (party) role. Moreover, a substantial minority of the freshmen took all three middle roles. Almost one-third (29%) were politico-neutral-nonpartisans prior to legislative service. While the odds against this are considerable, it is just about what one would expect from the proportion of freshman taking each middle role (.62 x .65 x .69 = .28). Certainly, in light of the fact that our freshmen-to-be had not yet had any legislative experience, one might reasonably expect that many would take a middle role either because of uncertainty or because of inconsistency.

Role Uncertainty. Most freshmen taking middle roles appear to have done so because of uncertainty. These respondents consistently responded to the role items with "don't know," "weak agree," or "weak disagree." Seventy-two percent of the politicos, eighty-four percent of the neutrals, and seventy percent of the nonpartisans were uncertain (see Table 5.2).[14] Not all freshmen-to-be taking middle roles were uncertain; sixteen to thirty percent (depending on role) were inconsistent. But, clearly, of those taking middle roles, a substantial majority did so due to uncertainty rather than inconsistency.

Nor can it be said that legislative experience markedly reduced this uncertainty—or at least the proportion of legislators who took the uncertain middle role(s). In fact, after a year's legislative ex-

Table 5.2: Initial Patterns of Uncertainty and Inconsistency*

	Politico (Representative)	Neutral (Interest Group)	Non-Partisan (Party)
Uncertain[a]	72%	84%	70%
Inconsistent[b]	28	16	30
N:	18	19	20

*See note 14.
a. Respondents would take two or three "middle" scale positions for each role item.
b. Respondents would take two or three polar scale positions for each role item.

perience, the percentages increased somewhat from one to eight points depending on roles (see Table 5.3). Another year's legislative experience tended to reduce uncertainty—but in only one case below what it had been prior to service. This finding has substantial importance. Since approximately two-thirds of the freshmen took middle roles sometime during the period under study, it appears that the traditional concern with polar roles may not be as significant as had once been assumed. The Burkean dilemma may be more dramatic, but compromise, inconsistency, and uncertainty appear to be more frequent (Tables 5.4, 5.5, and 5.6 summarize these patterns).

Middle Role Functions. Pre-legislative uncertainty might be explained by lack of knowledge about the legislative process compounded by the wisdom of caution. Pre-legislative inconsistency might be explained by the neophytes' inability to reconcile equally attractive alternatives. But what explains the continued high proportion of legislators occupying middle roles—particularly uncertain middle roles—after legislative experience? (See Table 5.7.) Moreover, comparison of freshman role positions with those of veterans reveals no substantial difference. Thus, what appears to be unlikely turns out to be usual in the California Assembly.

Certainly, if the legislator continually takes a middle position between polar roles (e.g., politico rather than either trustee or delegate) he or she may, simply, be compromising between the two. Wilder Crane suggested several years ago that all legislators are politicos, compromising between the delegate and trustee roles.[15] Thus, one explanation of the middle roles is that they are pragmatic—essentially political. Legislators respond to equally valid and attractive polar alternatives by taking a compromise position between them. Another explanation of the middle role is that it may be *transitional*. Might not legislative experience induce the lawmaker to change roles, for example, from partisan to antipartisan? In such a case, the middle role of nonpartisan could be transitional—a sort of "way station" during the change from one polar role to the other. Of course, it is also possible that the middle roles play more than one function at various times and in different situations.

Transition. For some legislators, the middle roles do appear to have been transitional as they moved from one polar role to the

Table 5.3: Uncertain and Inconsistent Middle Roles Over Time

Middle Roles:	Prior to Legislative Service	After One Year's Service	After Two Year's Service
Politico (Representative)			
Uncertain	72%	78%	88%
Inconsistent[a]	28	22	12
N:	18	18	16
Neutral (Interest Group)			
Uncertain	84%	92%	79%
Inconsistent[b]	16	8	21
N:	19	24	19
Non-partisan (Party)			
Uncertain	70%	71%	63%
Inconsistent[c]	30	29	36
N:	20	21	24

a. Respondents would take both Trustee and Delegate position.
b. Respondents would take both Facilitator and Resister position.
c. Respondents would take both Partisan and Anti-partisan position.

Table 5.4: Distribution of Representative Roles Over Time

	Distribution of Roles		
Role Category:	Prior to Legislative Service	After One Year's Service	After Two Year's Service
Trustee	10%	24%	35%
Politico	62	62	55
Delegate	28	14	10
Total	100	100	100
N:	29	29	29

Table 5.5: Distribution of Interest Group Roles Over Time

	Distribution of Roles		
Role Category:	Prior to Legislative Service	After One Year's Service	After Two Year's Service
Resister	7%	10%	21%
Neutral	65	83	66
Facilitator	28	7	14
Total	100	100	101*
N:	29	29	29

*Rounding error.

Table 5.6: Distribution of Party Roles Over Time

Role Category:	Prior to Legislative Service	After One Year's Service	After Two Year's Service
Anti-Partisan	7%	14%	3%
Non-Partisan	69	72	83
Partisan	24	14	14
Total	100	100	100
N:	29	29	29

Table 5.7: The Uncertain Middle Role Over Time

	Percentage of All Freshmen Taking the Uncertain Middle Role		
Role:	Before Legislative Experience	After One Year's Experience	After Two Year's Experience
Uncertain (Representative Role)	45%	48%	48%
Uncertain (Interest Group Role)	55	76	52
Uncertain (Party Role)	48	52	52

Table 5.8: Patterns of Role Acquisition

Acquisition Pattern:	Representational*	Interest Group	Party
CONSISTENT			
Polar[a]	11%	7%	3%
Middle[b]	32	48	38
TRANSITION[c]	32	28	14
COMPROMISE[d]	25	17	45
Total	100	100	100

*Percentages calculated on the base of 28 respondents. One freshman changed from Delegate to Trustee, but the change was so quick that we did not have a chance to observe him in what we suspect was his transitional middle role. This is the only case (our of 87) in which the role change was so rapid that we do not have a "picture" of the freshman's middle role.

a. **Consistent Polar** means that the freshman took the same polar role (Trustee or Delegate; Partisan or Anti-Partisan; Facilitator or Resister) at each of the three interviews.

b. **Consistent Middle** means that the freshman took a middle role (Politico, Neutral or Non-Partisan) at each of the three interviews.

c. **Transition** means that the freshman moved from a middle role to a polar role (e.g., Politico-to-Trustee) or from a polar role through a middle role to a polar role (e.g., Trustee-Politico-Delegate).

d. **Compromise** means that the freshman moved to a middle role, either from a polar role (e.g., Resister-Neutral) or from a middle role to a polar role and then back to a middle role (e.g., Nonpartisan to Partisan to Nonpartisan).

other. Nine freshmen (32%) appeared to have followed this path in arriving at their representational roles during their first term in office (see Table 5.8). Similarly, eight (28%) followed the transitional pattern in arriving at their interest-group roles; while four (14%) arrived at their party roles in this way.

Compromise. Other legislators began with polar roles, but apparently found them uncomfortable for one reason or another. As a result, they shifted to and stayed with middle roles. Instead of going *through* a middle role, these legislators went to and stayed with a middle role. Seven freshmen became politicos in this way (25%); five became neutrals (17%); and thirteen became nonpartisans (45%). An even larger percentage of freshmen started with middle roles and never left them. These, too, could be considered compromisers. Nine consistently played the politico role (32%); fourteen, the neutral role (48%); and eleven, the nonpartisan role (38%).

Role Change

Certainly, the substantial majority of freshmen taking middle roles, the relatively small number of freshmen taking polar roles, and the relatively small number who consistently kept any role for the entire period strongly suggests that the legislative roles initially taken by the freshmen-to-be were usually unstable. One way of illustrating this pattern of change is to diagram the role changes the freshmen took. Figures 5.1, 5.2, and 5.3 show the role change patterns which occurred during the freshmen's first term of legislative service. This is the period of time from our first interviews prior to election in 1966 through to the third interviews following reelection (Spring 1969). These figures omit the data from the second interviews and are, essentially, a simple "before and after" configuration.

During this period, there were two clearly discernible patterns of role change. For two role typologies, there was a net increase in freshmen taking polar roles. For the representational role, the trustee position became more popular, while the delegate became less popular (Figure 5.1). For the interest-group role, the resister, became more popular while the facilitator became less so (Figure 5.3). On the other hand, for the party role typology, both polar

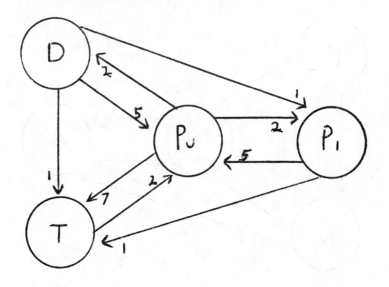

Role:	Gain	Loss	Net Change
T (Trustee)	9	2	+7
Pu (Politico-Uncertain)	12	11	+1
Pi (Politico-Inconsistent)	3	6	—3
D (Delegate)	2	7	—5

NOTE: Each circle symbolizes the designated role. The arrows indicate the direction of change. The numbers adjacent to the arrows indicate the number of freshmen changing roles. For example, in Figure 5.1, the arrow from circle "D" to circle "T" has the number "1" next to it. This means that during the first term, one freshman changed from the delegate to the trustee role. On the other hand, the arrow from "D" to "Pu" has a "5" which means that in the first term five freshmen changed from the delegate to the uncertain politico role. The table accompanying each figure summarizes the net change in the number of freshmen taking each role. For example, in Figure 5.1, the first term net decrease in freshmen taking the delegate role was five.

Figure 5.1: REPRESENTATIVE ROLE CHANGE PATTERNS
          (between first and third interview)

positions became less popular over time (Figure 5.2). In their first term, freshmen tended to move toward the nonpartisan position.

Apparently change was a function of both role and time. Freshmen were more inclined to change roles during the first year than during the second year. In the first year, there was a total of fifty role changes compared to thirty-three in the second year, a thirty-four percent decrease in the frequency of change. Also, freshmen were a little more likely to change some roles than others. Thirty-eight percent of the changes were in party role while thirty-one

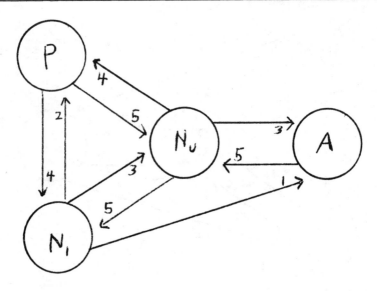

Role:	Gain	Loss	Net Change
P (Partisan)	6	9	−3
Nu (Non Partisan-Uncertain)	13	12	+1
Ni (Non Partisan-Inconsistent)	9	6	+3
A (Antipartisan)	4	5	−1

Figure 5.2: PARTY ROLE CHANGE PATTERNS (between first and third interview)

percent were in representational role and thirty percent in interest-group role.

More role change occurred in regard to the uncertain middle roles than any other—regardless of role typology. A quick look at Figures 5.1, 5.2, and 5.3 reveals the *central* position of the uncertain middle roles. Forty-six percent of all interest-group role changes involved the uncertain neutral role; forty-four percent of all representational role changes involved the uncertain politico role, and thirty-nine percent of all party role changes involved the uncertain nonpartisan role.

However, while these data reveal some of the function of role change, they do not explain the initial roles taken by freshmen-to-be—or their initial pre-legislative role sources.

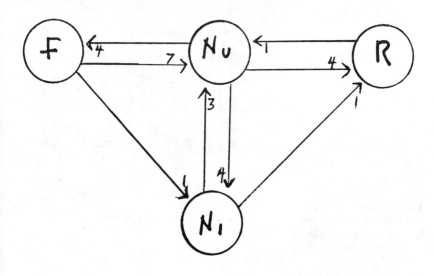

Role:	Gain	Loss	Net Change
R (Resister)	5	1	+4
Nu (Neutral-Uncertain)	11	12	—1
Ni (Neutral-Inconsistent)	5	4	+1
f (Facilitator)	4	8	—4

Figure 5.3: INTEREST-GROUP ROLE CHANGE PATTERNS
(between first and third interviews)

Pre-Legislative Role Sources

One of the major goals of this study was to determine when legislators' role orientations developed and what factors appear important in shaping them.

Sources. In order to examine possible pre-legislative sources of legislative roles, respondents were asked questions about (1) their individual backgrounds, (2) community involvement, and (3) previous political activities. (These data were gathered prior to legislative service and, in most cases, before election to office.) Twenty-five pre-legislative independent variables were measured and correlated to legislative roles. The data below (Table 5.9) reveal that only a handful of pre-legislative (or nonlegislative) variables associated with roles examined.

Examination of the first section of the table, "Residential and Community Life," reveals that only two of the correlations were

Table 5.9: Pre-Legislative Sources of Initial Legislative Role Orientations

Experience	With Representational Role (Trustee)	With Interest Group Role (Facilitator)	With Party Role (Anti-Partisan)	N	(P = Pearsonian) (B = Biserial)
	Strength of Association				Correlation Used
Residential and Community Life					
Years lived in area	.305	−.086	.022	31	P
Years at present address	.296	−.100	.131	31	P
Number of memberships in community organizations	.278	.364*	.213	31	P
Number of community organization meetings attended per month	−.058	−.013	.031	31	P
Officer in one or more community organizations	−.394*	.256	.043	30	B
Political Activities					
Active in other (earlier) campaigns	.603*a	.005	.122	31	B
Member of a volunteer political organization	.438*	.165	.167	31	B
Active in a volunteer political organization	.351*	−.584*	.175	31	B
Active in a volunteer political organization (members only)	.072	−.612*	−.080	21	B
Have given money to other (earlier) campaigns	.333	−.063	.037	31	B
Had previously run for public office	.575*	−.007	−.059	31	B
Had previously held public office	.603*	−.221	.017	31	B
Affiliated with Democratic Party	.289	−.254	.011	31	B
Age of first adult political activity	−.136	.127	−.280	31	P
Ideology (liberal)**	.069	.009	.160	25	P

Table 5.9 (Continued)

Personal Background					
Age	−.111	.125	−.283	31	P
High School Graduate***	.000	.000	.000	30	B
College Graduate	.366*	**.508***	**−.625***	31	B
Post Graduage college work	.040	.194	.096	30	B
Occupation requires college education	−.147	.000	.166	31	B
Has followed one life occupation only	.081	.101	.112	31	B
Social Class (subjective)	.340	.201	.120	31	P
Present Status (subjective)	−.049	−.048	−.162	31	P
Status Aspiration (subjective)	.081	−.370*	−.275	29	P
Aspiration gap (aspiration minus present)	.087	−.081	.076	29	P

*Statistically significant at $p \leqslant .05$.
a. Correlations in bold face are = $r^2 \geqslant .200$.
** Determined by use of a nine-point liberal-conservative scale.
***All respondents had graduated from high school.

statistically significant, and that neither was strong enough to explain much variance.[16] For example, having been an officer in one or more community organizations appears to be only slightly associated with playing the delegate role ($r^2 = .155$).[17]

Legislators' political activity prior to serving in the Assembly appears to have been the richest source of pre-legislative role orientations. This is particularly true for the representative role, where three moderately strong correlations met our definition of meaningful ($r^2 \geqslant .200$). These three variables were: (1) activity in other (earlier) campaigns; (2) having previously held elective office; and (3) having previously run for public office. One other variable correlated strongly enough with interest-group role to be considered meaningful. Playing the resister interest-group role was moderately associated with being *active* in a volunteer political organization. Since *membership per se* in a volunteer political organization was not meaningfully associated with the interest-group role, our findings suggest that it is activity rather than membership which is significant. Finally, and perhaps most interesting of all, none of the measures of political activity was associated in any meaningful way with party role.

The third area of pre-legislative experience, "Personal Background," reveals only two substantial correlations. The patterns of association are as interesting as are their strengths. All three roles correlated with "college graduation" at statistically significant levels. For two roles, the association was moderately substantial, playing the facilitator role ($r^2 = .258$) and playing the partisan role ($r^2 = .391$). These findings are similar to those of Wahlke and colleagues, who also found that education was associated with interest-group role orientations.[18] Yet association with the trustee role, while statistically significant, was hardly meaningful ($r^2 = .134$). Perhaps of greater interest was the fact that, of the twenty-five pre-legislative variables examined, only "college graduation" was associated in a statistically significant way with all three roles.

Interestingly, of twenty-five pre-legislative life variables examined, fifteen *did not* associate in a statistically significant level with any role. Four other variable correlations, while statistically significant, were not strong enough to be considered meaningfully associated. *Only six variables* were meaningfully associated with one or more roles.

Representational Roles. Only one of the three roles—representative—appears to have been rooted to any great extent in pre-legislative life experience, most of which appears to have been political in nature. Interestingly, political activity did not associate meaningfully with party role. Apparently, political activity at the local level does not orient the candidate to play any particular party role in the California Assembly.

Party Roles. For such variables as "having run for public office" and "having held public office," the lack of correlation to party role is not hard to explain. California local government has been nonpartisan for over fifty years. City councilmen, school board members, or county supervisors seldom become identified with, much less involved in, partisan politics unless they actually run for a partisan office. As Charles Adrian suggests, partisan politics is often dysfunctional for the holder of a nonpartisan office.[19] On the other hand, the fact that partisan activists, those who were active members of volunteer political groups, failed to take any predictable party role is surprising. One could reasonably expect that those who had been active in such volunteer party organizations as the California Democratic Council or the United Republicans of California would be quite partisan in their legislative role orientation. The fact that they were not suggests that perhaps the nonpartisan image of the California legislature had more to do with freshmen-elect party role orientations than did the experience of partisan political activity. Until quite recently, California's legislature has had a minimal partisan atmosphere.[20] As one astute observer of state legislatures recently commented, the typical California legislator could legitimately think of him- or herself as a nonpartisan.[21] Another, earlier, writer suggested twenty years ago that the successful office holder in California could well ignore the party by building a private organization, keeping a personal "war chest," and running his or her own campaign.[22] Indicative of this nonpartisan attitude is the fact that California's Assembly members (both freshmen and veterans) ranked the state's political parties as only moderately significant in the legislative process—far less important than the Speaker, committees, interest groups, or the governor, (see Table 6.1).[23] On the other hand, Bruce Robeck reports that, in January 1967 (at the time of our study) eighty-three percent of California legislators interviewed rated parties as "very important" or "important."[24] It is significant, however, to note that, of about two thousand bills introduced in each legislative session, fewer than four hundred produce any appreciable party differences.

Interest-Group Roles. Turning to the roots of interest-group roles, Ronald Hedlund, in his Iowa study, suggests that those legislators with a better than average knowledge of lobbyists are more likely to be favorably inclined toward them than are those who have less knowledge.[25] In addition, Wahlke has suggested that a legislator's receptivity to interest groups will be associated with his general evaluation of pressure politics as a mode of political activity.[26] These two suggestions raise some interesting questions worth examining. Were California legislators-to-be more likely to be facilitators if they were knowledgeable about interest groups? And were those legislators-to-be who were "group"-oriented in politics more likely to be facilitators than those who were "individual"-oriented?

During our interviews, each respondent was asked, "To your knowledge, which interest groups are most influential in California at the present time?" Only two legislators-to-be volunteered the name(s) of a lobbyist; nine named a specific statewide lobby—e.g., COPE, Merchants and Manufacturers, California Teachers Association, etc.; while fifteen made some kind of generalized reference to some group—e.g., the "church," "labor," or "teachers," etc. Three could not think of any answer, while two said "newspapers." Clearly, even after giving these legislative candidates the benefit of the doubt, we must conclude that most were either not too well-informed about the myriad interest groups in the state or were almost uniformly unwilling to answer the question. While we recognize that the area of interest-group activity is a sensitive one for most candidates and office holders, the overwhelming proportion of uninformed answers appears to suggest that our respondents were not able to answer the question because they were not very knowledgeable about interest groups in California rather than because the question was sensitive. Thus, unfortunately, no sophisticated measure of interest-group information was possible. However, by categorizing our legislators-to-be as above average, average, and below average in information, we could make an acceptable though crude categorization of levels of information. We found no relationship (gamma = .097) between levels of information about interest groups and interest-group roles played by California legislators-to-be. While our data do not directly contradict Hedlund's findings, they do suggest that any relationship between information and role is probably a product of legislative service rather than life experience prior to serving in a legislative body. We suggest that this may be a function of the paucity of information which nonincumbent candidates have about interest groups.[27]

We were also interested in testing Wahlke's "group politics" hypothesis. One item in the interest-group role battery and one item in the party role battery were identical in stating an alternative between group political action and individual political action. They were:

(1) Under our form of government, every individual should take an interest in government directly, not through a political party.

(2) Under our form of government, every individual should take an interest in government directly, not through interest-group organizations.

Agreement with these two items indicated that the legislator favored individual political action; disagreement indicated that he or she favored group action. By combining these two role items, we were able to construct a crude "group saliency index." The correlation between this index and the interest-group role score revealed a substantial association between the two (gamma = .795). Unfortunately, there is a methodological problem involved in this procedure because the interest-group role item cited above (number 2) is both a part of the group saliency index (half of it) and the interest-group role score (a third of it). In order to eliminate the effects of this, we compared only the party group item above (number 1) with the interest-group role scores. As a result, we found a reduced but still substantial association (gamma = .590) which suggests that facilitators view group action more favorably than do resisters. Thus, our data show a moderate association between the way a legislator-to-be viewed group politics and his or her initial interest-group role.

Role Systems

Intrarole Correlations. Another way of assessing the source of legislative roles is to sort out the pre-legislative causes from the legislative causes. While we have looked at some *specific* pre-legislative sources in the previous section, we obviously have not looked at all or, in all probability, even most of them. For example, we did not attempt to relate personality structure to legislative roles. Obviously, we have not and could not identify or measure all the potential pre-legislative sources of role orientations. But we can measure the association between pre-legislative roles and roles assumed after legislative service. For example, if we find that legislators' party roles before legislative service are exactly the same as their party roles after legislative service, we could reasonably assert that legislative service had no impact on this role and that pre-legislative experience had everything to do with it. (Or, at the most, legislative experience simply reinforced the pre-existing role orientation.) If, on the other hand, we find no relationship between role before and after legislative experience, we could then assert that the influence of pre-legislative life had been totally eliminated and that legislative service was the complete source of role orientation. Of course, neither situation is likely to occur; but if we can determine what proportion of each

Table 5.10: Intra-Role Correlations

Role Before Service	Role After the First Term
Representative	.705
Interest Group	.267
Party	.294

Table 5.11: Explained Variance Between Roles

Role Before Service	Role After the First Term
Representative	50%
Interest Group	7
Party	9

Table 5.12

Intra-Role Correlations	Role After 1 Year	Role After 2 Years
A. Representative		
Pre-Service	.713	.705
Role After 1 Year		.867
B. Interest Group		
Pre-Service Role	.311	.267
Role After 1 Year		.572
C. Party		
Pre-Service	.274	.294
Role After 1 Year		.700

Table 5.13: Role Networks[*]

	Interest Group	Party
I. Prior to legislative experience		
Representative	.115	−.112
Interest Group		.627
II. After one year's legislative experience		
Representative	−.044	−.143
Interest Group		.144
III. After two year's legislative experience		
Representative	.337	−.079
Interest Group		.248

*By Spearman rank correlation.

legislative role is produced by legislative experience, we can reasonably attribute the remainder to pre-legislative life experience.

Table 5.10 presents the intrarole correlations for the three roles examined. Table 5.11 presents the r^2 values in the same format to assist the reader in assessing the relative impact of pre-legislative and legislative life upon legislative roles. Succinctly stated, pre-legislative life had little to do with explaining the interest group and party roles played by legislators at the end of their first term. On the other hand, half the legislators' representational role was rooted in his pre-legislative experience.

Of equal interest is the fact that other data strongly suggest that, by the end of the first term, the legislators' representational role is rather firmly established, but party and interest-group roles are still shaky.

The tabulations in Table 5.12A reveal consistently high correlations between representational roles at all three points in time. This strongly suggests not only substantial roots in pre-legislative life but a high level of role stability. On the other hand, Tables 5.12B and 5.12C reveal lower intrarole correlations for both the interest-group and party roles. Certainly, the correlation between roles at the end of the term and after one year's service are high enough (.572 and .700) to suggest a developing stability. But the fact that these roles have developed almost totally as a result of two years' service as a freshman legislator also suggests that subsequent substantial role change could be reasonably expected.

Interrole Correlations. Wahlke et al. have suggested that there is a role network, that the roles which a legislator plays are interrelated. However, our data do not show this. Prior to legislative experience, there was a meaningful relationship between party and interest-group roles (r_s = .627) with facilitators tending to be partisans and resisters tending to be antipartisans. However, as can be seen in Table 5.13, there were no other meaningful interrole associations at any time, either before or after legislative experience. This may be due in part to the unsettled nature of the interest-group and party roles observed above. But, since even in change there was no correlation, it appears that there is no essential association between roles established after two years' legislative experience.

Summary

We have traced and analyzed the development and changes in legislative roles from a point in time prior to any legislative experience through the first term of office past reelection and into the beginning of the second term. In some instances, our findings are supportive of other studies and in other instances they are in contradiction.

Our first finding is that most California freshmen entered the Assembly with middle role orientations. This substantial proportion did not change much during the first term. Most freshmen taking these middle roles were uncertain in their positions prior to legislative experience and after the first term. In one case, a smaller percentage of freshmen took polar party roles (partisan or antipartisan) at the beginning of their second term than had taken them prior to legislative experience. Significantly, the number of uncertain middle roles was so great that they constituted an absolute majority for two role typologies—interest-group and party—and were almost a majority of the representational roles (48%).

Middle roles appear to serve both transitional and compromise functions. In particular, the nonpartisan party role, occupied by eighty-three percent of the legislators at the beginning of their second term, appears as a compromise between the polar alternatives. On the other hand, the patterns of change suggest that the middle representational role (politico) was more transitional. Thus, at the present time—our data conform more with the positions of Wilder Crane and Ken Janda than those of Wahlke et al. or Frank J. Sorauf.

Pre-legislative life experiences were not meaningfully associated with the three roles considered except in a relatively few cases. The exceptions were those involving political experiences which tended to be associated with representational roles. Education was also associated with all three roles. Clearly, however, the kinds of pre-legislative experience examined were not associated with legislative roles to the extent that we had originally anticipated.

We discovered that initial party and interest-group roles were not associated with those taken subsequently. We also found representational roles were substantially associated over time. In fact, about half the subsequent representational roles could be attributed to pre-legislative life. To be sure, we could not identify or measure all aspects of pre-legislative life. But the consistently high correlations between representational roles over time strongly suggest that this was the most stable and consistent role examined and that it does have meaningful roots in pre-legislative life. On the other hand, party and interest group roles were clearly a product of legislative life. There is some suggestion that both party and interest group roles were somewhat stabilized by the end of the first term. It is significant that the twenty-nine freshmen experienced fifty role changes in their first year compared to thirty-three in the second year. This decrease in role change frequency suggests an increasing stabilization of roles over time as a result of legislative experience.

Finally, we found that there was no meaningful association between roles after legislative experience. The one meaningful association between party and interest-group roles which existed prior to legislative service later disappeared. These findings suggest that the three roles are not interrelated. Thus, the individual lawmaker can change one legislative role orientation without any undue stress being placed on the other roles.[28]

NOTES

1. Ralph Linton, *The Study of Man* (New York: Appleton-Century, 1936) and see also his *The Cultural Background of Personality* (New York: Appleton-Century, 1945). For a review of definitions of role, see Lionel J. Neiman and James W. Hughes, "The Problem of the Concept of Role—A Re-Survey of the Literature," *Social Forces* XXX (December 1951), pp. 141-149.

2. C. H. Cooley, *Human Nature and the Social Order* (New York: Scribner's, 1902); and J. L. Moreno, *Who Shall Survive?* (Washington, D.C.: Nervous and Mental Disease Publications, 1934).

3. Eugene L. and Ruth E. Hartley, *Fundamentals of Social Psychology* (New York: Knopf, 1955), p. 486. See also Neal Gross et al., *Explorations in Role Analysis* (New York: John Wiley, 1958); and Bruce J. Beddle and Edwin J. Thomas, eds., *Role Theory* (New York: John Wiley, 1966).

4. Gross et al., op. cit.

5. Linton, op. cit., p. 113.

6. John C. Wahlke et al., *The Legislative System* (New York: John Wiley, 1962), p. 9.

7. A partial list of studies of representational role would include Wahlke et al., op. cit.; Allan Kornberg, "Perception and Constituency Influence on Legislative Behavior,"

Western Political Quarterly XIX (June 1966), pp. 285-292; Wilder W. Crane, Jr., *The Legislative Struggle in Wisconsin: Decision Making in the 1957 Wisconsin General Assembly* (Madison: Ph.D. dissertation, 1959); Eulau, op. cit.; Ronald D. Hedlund, "Legislative Socialization and Role Orientations," The Laboratory for Political Research, University of Iowa, Report 11, October 1967; and J. Roland Pennock, "Political Representation: An Overview," in *Representation,* J. Roland Pennock and John W. Chapman, eds. (New York: Atherton Press, 1968), pp. 3-27.

Studies of interest-group role would include Wahlke et al., op. cit.; Henry Teune, "Legislative Attitudes Toward Interest Groups," *Midwest Journal of Political Science* XI (November 1967), pp. 489-504; Wilder W. Crane, Jr., "A Test of Effectiveness of Interest Group Pressure on Legislators," *Southwest Social Science Quarterly,* LI (1960), pp. 335-340; and John C. Wahlke et al., "American State Legislators' Role Orientations Toward Pressure Groups," *Journal of Politics* XXII (May 1960), pp. 203-227.

Studies of party role include Patterson, op. cit.; William M. Buchanan, *Legislative Partisanship,* (Berkeley: University of California Press, 1963); Frank J. Sorauf, *Party and Representation* (New York: Atherton Press, 1963); and Wahlke et al., op. cit.

Studies of bureaucratic role orientations include Hallie Farmer, *The Legislative Process in Alabama* (Bureau of Public Administration: University of Alabama Press, 1949); Willard C. Havard and Loren T. Beth, *The Politics of Misrepresentation* (Baton Rouge, La.: University of Louisiana Press, 1962); and George A. Bell and Evelyn L. Wentworth, *The Legislative Process in Maryland,* (College Park: University of Maryland Press, 1958).

Studies of purposive roles include William M. Buchanan, "The Legislator as a Specialist," *Western Political Quarterly* XIII (September 1960), pp. 636-651; Barber, op. cit.; Wahlke et al., op. cit.; and Oliver Garceau and Corrinne Silverman, "A Pressure Group and the pressured: A Case Report," *American Political Science Review* XLVIII (June 1954), pp. 422-426.

8. Wayne L. Francis, "The Role Concept in Legislatures," *Journal of Politics,* XXCII (August 1965), pp. 567-585.

9. See, for example, Cleo H. Cherryholmes and Michael J. Shapiro, *Representatives and Roll Calls* (Indianapolis: Bobbs-Merrill, 1969), in which they consider several variables which are predictive of roll call behavior.

10. Kenneth Janda, "Some Theory and Data on Representational Roles and Legislative Behavior," unpublished manuscript.

11. See Wahlke et al., op. cit., pp. 272-280, 325, 259-264.

12. Wayne Francis suggests that it is useful to think of role as a unidimensional continuum. See Wayne Francis, op. cit., pp. 569-570.

13. See Wahlke op. cit., p. 23. It should be noted that Wahlke suggests pre-legislative experience as one of four possible sources of legislative roles. The other three are: (1) formal enactments (constitutions, statutes, etc.); (2) organization and structure (number of chambers, size of each, staffing, etc.); and (3) experience in role.

14. Definitions of "inconsistent" and "uncertain" were based on the frequency with which each middle role respondent gave polar role answers to the role items. Those giving two or three conflicting polar role responses were categorized as inconsistent. Those giving none or one were categorized as uncertain. It should not be too surprising that some freshmen legislators are inconsistent in their response to the role items. The polar alternatives are both legitimate and attractive.

15. See Wilder W. Crane, Jr., *The Legislative Struggle in Wisconsin: Decision Making in the 1957 Wisconsin Assembly,* (Madison: University of Wisconsin, 1959), passim.

16. Since our sample approximates the universe (thirty-one of thirty-three fresh-

men) statistical significance appears to be of little consequence for the data under consideration. However, we have indicated those correlations and percentages which are statistically significant for those who are interested.

17. We have used the simple concept of explained variance, arbitrarily picking twenty percent as the critical value. Thus a correlation of .448 (.448^2 = .200) became the critical correlation value. This means that we reject any correlation below .448 as being too weak to explain much. For a discussion of this technique, see Linton C. Freeman, *Elementary Applied Statistics* (New York: John Wiley, 1968), pp. 101-106.

18. Wahlke op. cit., p. 330.

19. Charles R. Adrian, "Some General Characteristics of Non-partisan Elections," *American Political Science Review* XLVI (September 1952). On the other hand, partisan division within local nonpartisan city councils may be the basis for conflict. See Robert J. Huckshorn and Charles E. Young, "Study of Voting Splits on City Councils in Los Angeles County," *Western Political Quarterly* XIII (June 1960), pp. 494-496.

20. In fact, campaigning for public office in California had little partisan flavor to it until the early 1950s.

21. William Buchanan, *Legislative Partisanship: The Deviant Case* (Berkeley and Los Angeles: University of California Press, 1963), p. 138.

22. Mary Ellen Leary, San Francisco *News,* March 7, 1949, cited in Buchanan, op. cit., p. 138.

23. Data originally presented in a paper, "Consensus and Polarization of Freshmen Legislators' Attitudes," Charles G. Bell and Charles M. Price, Western Political Science Association annual convention, Seattle, Washington, March 1968.

24. Bruce Robeck, "Legislative Partisanship Constituency and Malapportionment," *American Political Science Review,* LXVI (December 1972), p. 1248.

25. Ronald D. Hedlund, "Legislative Socialization and Role Orientations," Report 11, Laboratory for Political Research, Department of Political Science, University of Iowa, October 1967, p. 19. Also, see Harmon Zeigler and Michael Baer, *Lobbying* (Belmont, Calif.: Wadsworth, 1969).

26. Wahlke, op. cit., p. 324.

27. However, it should be noted that having held local elective office was not associated with interest-group role either (see Table 5.9).

28. It is interesting to note that the freshman-elect role stability is at the same low level as that of the general public's issue stability. See Philip E. Converse, "The Nature of Belief Systems in Mass Publics," *Ideology and Discontent,* David E. Apter, ed. (New York: Free Press, 1966), pp. 238-245.

Chapter 6

CONSENSUS AND POLARIZATION OF

FRESHMAN LEGISLATORS' ATTITUDES

Introduction

The norms, attitudes, values, and perceptions shared by legislators are significant in the operation of a legislature, and certainly how and when legislators acquire these traits is highly significant. It would seem likely that, just as "folkways" or "rules of the game" come to be commonly shared by legislators, so too would their perceptions about legislative "inputs"—the various factors in the legislative process—come to be commonly held. However, while much scholarly work has been devoted to studying folkways and rules of the game, little research effort has been devoted to the kinds of legislative input perceptions which we will be discussing in this chapter.

It is our intention in this chapter: (1) to look at certain perceptions which freshman legislators bring to their lawmaking tasks; (2) to analyze the changes which occur in these perceptions, and, (3) to determine, hopefully, some of the roots of these changes. Studies by John Wahlke et al., Kenneth Prewitt et al., Ronald

Hedlund, and others have clearly documented some process of legislative socialization. It would be fair to infer from their studies that the legislative experience exerts a meaningful influence on legislators' perceptions relative to their common concerns.[1] Yet, a pioneering study by Herbert McClosky, Paul J. Hoffman, and Rosemary O'Hara raises the interesting possibility that there may often be more polarization of attitudes and perceptions than consensus in legislatures.[2] This idea has merit, in that legislators, unlike members of most groups, achieve membership as a result of conflict; also, because legislative bodies are to some extent structured for internal conflict.[3] Some internal sources of conflict are, for example: election of the speaker and selection of committee chairmen, the conduct of committee hearings in an adversary atmosphere, the allocation of scarce resources, and, of course, the very act of voting. In addition, of course, constituency differences provide external sources of conflict. Thus, while legislative experience may produce agreement concerning some attitudes, it may also be that it produces disagreement, even polarization about other facets of the legislative process such as: policy alternatives, the importance of given events, or the significance of various inputs.

To test the incidence of legislative socialization in regard to perceptions of inputs, the following hypotheses were posited:

(1) freshmen perceptions will become more like those of the veterans, over time; and

(2) the range of freshman perceptions about any particular input will become smaller, over time.

Method

The data in this chapter are drawn from all three freshmen panels, as well as the single set of interviews with veterans. In each of the four panels questions were included about twenty-one selected legislative inputs (e.g., the governor, the Speaker, interest groups, or local political leaders). Each respondent was asked: "Using this self-anchoring scale, how much influence (in the legislature) do you think _____ has?" (See the appendices for the questionnaires.)

0	1	2	3	4	5	6

Not at all
Significant

Very
Significant

Figure 6.1.

Findings

PERCEPTIONS OF INFLUENCE

First, mean average "perception of influence scores" were cal-culated for each of the twenty-one inputs for each of the four interview panels. The higher the mean score, the more influential it was perceived to be. (All mean scores are listed for each input for each panel in Table 6.1). For example, the Speaker was con-sistently perceived by all panels to be the most influential of the legislative inputs considered. On the other hand, the freshmen class of '66 changed its perceptions about the least influential in-put. Prior to service, they perceived the conflict between city and suburb to be least influential, while after a year's service they gave two other inputs that distinction (local business leaders and local labor leaders). Finally, after their second year of service, they settled on local labor leaders as being least influential. While it is interesting to observe the changes in perceptions, it is more impor-tant, for our purposes, to consider the reasons for those changes— to see if they are a manifestation of legislative socialization. These changes are summarized in Table 6.2.

Perceptual Change

One may look at the data in Table 6.2 in several ways. First, consideration should be given to *net changes* in perception scores during the first term. For some perceptions the net change was quite substantial, such as the governor's influence. (The net change for each perception was ranked. Those changes ranking in the top third were defined as *substantial;* middle third were defined as *moderate;* and bottom third were defined as *negligible.*) For others,

Table 6.1: Perceptions of Input Influence Held by Freshman and Veteran Legislators

Input Factor	Panel Averages				Panel Rankings			
	I*	II**	III***	Vets****	I	II	III	Vets
North v. South	3.16	3.06	2.26	2.34	14	16	20	19
Urban v. Rural	4.00	3.87	3.65	2.66	9	7.5	11	15
City v. Suburb	2.55	2.50	2.47	2.19	21	19	18	21
City Government	2.94	3.10	3.19	3.70	18	15	14	8
County Government	3.52	3.16	2.87	3.56	12	14	16	11
Local Business Leaders	2.58	2.26	2.41	2.60	20	20.5	19	16
Local Labor Leaders	3.06	2.26	2.19	2.68	16.5	20.5	21	17
Local Community Leaders	2.90	2.87	2.90	2.77	19	17	15	14
Local Political Leaders	3.06	2.61	3.20	2.52	16.5	18	13	18
State Political Parties	3.57	3.34	3.96	3.00	11	12	9	13
Minority Leader	4.10	3.87	4.19	4.25	6	7.5	7	6
Speaker	5.48	5.75	5.30	5.81	1	1	1	1
Committees	4.83	5.38	5.09	4.78	2	2	2	3
Committee Chairmen	4.71	4.34	4.63	4.54	3	5	5	5
Governor	3.68	4.51	4.70	4.71	10	4	4	4
State Bureaucracy	4.03	3.86	4.00	3.29	8	9	8	12
State Senate	4.40	4.64	4.96	5.16	4	3	3	2
Federal Government	4.28	3.37	3.40	2.31	5	11	12	20
Interest Groups	4.06	4.03	4.33	3.83	7	6	6	7
Parliamentary Procedure	3.07	3.33	2.86	3.66	15	13	17	9.5
Each Legislator's Own Ideology	3.25	3.62	3.67	3.64	13	10	10	9.5

*Freshmen interviewed prior to service (Panel 1).
**Freshmen interviewed after one year's service (Panel 2).
***Freshmen interviewed after two year's service (Panel 3).
****Veteran Interviews

the net change was negligible, such as for perceptions of the influence of local community leaders. The net change in perceptions is one way to measure the result of two years of legislative experience.

Second, another measure is the *gross change* in perception scores. This measure gives us a better idea of the totality of changes which take place when such changes are in different directions during the first and second years of legislative experience. For example, the net change in perceptions of the influence of state political parties is only moderate (.39 points). But the gross change is substantial (.85). The difference between net (.39) and gross (.85) change is a product of both a *decrease* of .23 points in

Table 6.2: Changes in Perception Scores

	Changes During First Year	Changes During Second Year	Changes During Complete Term	
			Net	Gross
Governor	.83	.19	1.02	1.02
North v. South	−.10	−.80	−.90	.90
Federal Government	−.91	.03	−.88	.94
Local Labor Leaders	−.80	−.07	−.87	.87
County Government	−.36	−.29	−.65	.65
State Senate	.24	.39	.56	.56
Ideology	.37	.05	.42	.42
State Political Parties	−.23	.62	.39	.85
Urban v. Rural	−.13	−.22	−.35	.35
Interest Groups	−.03	.30	.27	.33
Committees	.55	−.29	.26	.84
City Government	.16	.09	.25	.25
Parliamentary Procedure	.26	−.47	−.21	.73
Speaker	.27	−.45	−.18	.72
Local Business Leaders	−.32	.15	−.17	.47
Local Political Leaders	−.45	.59	.14	1.04
Minority Leader	−.23	.32	.09	.55
Committee Chairmen	−.37	.29	−.08	.66
City v. Suburb	−.05	−.02	−.07	.07
State Bureaucracy	−.17	.14	−.03	.31
Local Community Leaders	−.03	.03	∅	.06
Average	±.33	±.28	±.37	

the first year and an increase of .62 in the second year (net = .62 − .23 = .39; but gross = .62 + .23 = .85).

Third, whether one looks at net or gross change the *period of change* should also be considered. For example, the change in perceptions of the influence of the federal government took place substantially in the first year (a drop of .91 points), while the change in the perceptions of the conflict between North and South occurred largely in the second year (a drop of .80 points). (The conflicts between Northern and Southern California have been considered by most political observers as both substantial and significant. Until court-ordered reapportionment, this conflict was institutionalized in the legislature—the Senate being controlled by Northern California and the Assembly by the South. North-South differences can be seen in the allocation of some tax funds, voting patterns, party organization, and in the numerous attempts to divide California into two states.) Other changes took place at a relatively equal pace over both years, for example, the steadily decreasing importance attributed to county government (a drop of .36 points in the first year and .29 points in the second year). Finally, highlighting the difference between net and gross change discussed above, some perceptions moved in opposite directions in the two years under examination. Thus, perceptions of committee influence increased by .55 points in the first year and dropped by .29 points in the second. Several factors probably account for these various patterns. We would like to suggest three such factors: (1) *debunking* of common political myths; (2) discovery of the significance of *unsuspected* legislative factors; and (3) *delayed* (or cyclical) recognition of the *importance of re-election.*

Debunking Common Political Myths. Freshmen Assembly members soon discovered that their perceptions of influence were in some cases overinflated. The most striking changes which occurred during the first year were sharp reductions in perceptions of the influence of the federal government (−.91 points) and local labor leaders (−.80 points). The perceptual change for the federal government is particularly significant, and it reduced its rank importance from fifth to eleventh (see Table 6.1). And, during the second year of legislative service, freshman perceptions of the influence of the conflict between North and South was substantially reduced (−.80 points).

Unsuspected Legislative Factors. Freshmen entering the legislative process soon discovered that the governor was considerably more influential than they had originally thought. Initially, they had accorded him a moderately important role (score of 3.68, ranked tenth). After one year, the governor ranked fourth, lower only than the Speaker, committees and the state Senate. The freshmen also discovered that the other house, the state Senate, was more influential than they had first thought. This change occurred more evenly over both years. Finally, they discovered rather quickly that each legislator's own ideology was more important than originally anticipated.

Getting Reelected. During their first year of service, freshmen did not consider state political parties or local political leaders as very important (ranked twelfth and eighteenth, respectively).

However, after having run for reelection, their perceptions of these two factors increased substantially.

Veterans' Influence. Another way of assessing the overall process of perception change is to calculate the correlation between freshmen's and veterans' perceptions, both before the freshmen had served in the legislature and after they had served two years. The correlation between initial freshman-to-be perceptions and those of veterans was a moderately strong .650. After two years' service, the correlation increased to a stronger .809. (We are assuming that veterans' perceptions were relatively stable over the period of three years, 1966-1969.)

However, before one sees in this trend confirmation of the hypothesis, it will be instructive to consider the implication of the initial correlation. The correlation of perceptions between veterans and freshmen-to-be was .650. Clearly, these legislators-to-be in the prepatory legislative socialization phase had a set of perceptions which were not vastly different from those held by the veterans. Thus, it is not surprising that, after two years of legislative service, the correlation between veterans and freshmen should have become stronger, increasing to .809. In a rough way (using the r^2 technique), we can say that, after two years of legislative experience, about twenty percent of freshman perceptions appear to have been the product of legislative experience. (This figure is derived by subtracting the square of .650 from the square of .809 $[(.809)^2 - (.650)^2]$ which equals .23 or 23%.)

Another way to test for the existence of socialization is to determine if freshman input perceptions change over time *toward* those of the veterans. For ten of the inputs, there appears to have been a trend in freshman perceptions toward those of the veterans. But for ten other perceptions, the trend was divergent! (For one input, there was no change in perceptions.) At first glance, this certainly offers no support for the primary hypothesis. However, a careful examination of the data raises an interesting possibility. Perhaps the dynamic of socialization is partially a function of the "gap" or differences in perception. As can be seen in Table 6.1, there were marked differences between initial freshman perceptions and veteran perceptions for some items. For example, the difference between the initial freshman and veteran perceptions about the influence of the federal government was a substantial

1.97 points (4.28 − .2.31); for the urban-rural conflict, the gap was
1.34; and for the governor it was 1.03. In each of these cases,
freshman perceptions moved closer to the veterans' after two years
of legislative experience. On the other hand, there was almost no
difference between initial freshmen's perceptions and those of
veterans regarding the influence of local business leaders, county
government, or committees. Interestingly, for these three inputs,
the trend among freshmen was away from veterans' perceptions.
Table 6.3 illustrates that, when the initial perceptual gap was
greater than average, the trend was usually (67%) *toward* veterans'
perceptions. However, when the initial gap was smaller than
average, the trend was usually (70%) *away* from the veterans'
perceptions. Another way of expressing the relationship is to state
that the association between the size of initial perceptual gap and
the trend was a moderately strong .648.[4]

Another clue to the dynamics of legislative socialization may be
found in the relationship between the time of greatest perception
change and the observed trend toward or away from veteran perceptions. In some cases, perceptions changed most during the first
year of legislative experience. For example, freshman perceptions
of the influence of local labor leaders dropped by .80 points
during the first year. During the second year, the drop was only
.07 points. Clearly, the major change in this perception occurred
during the first year. Similarly, perception of the influence of the
governor increased by .83 points in the first year, but only .19 in
the second; changes in the perception of the influence of the
federal government dropped .91 points in the first year, but in-

Table 6.3: Perceptual Gap and Trend Relationships Between Freshmen and
Veterans

	Initial Perceptual Differences	
Freshman Perceptual Change	Greater than $\overline{X}$*	Less than $\overline{X}$
Toward Veteran Perceptions	67%	30%
Away from Veteran Perceptions	33%	70%
N:**	9	10
		G = .648

*$\overline{X}$ is defined as the median change value.
**The median change value and another value which did not change have not been
included.

creased a negligible .03 points in the second year. It is reasonable to assert that in these—and in like cases—the impact of legislative socialization was most substantial during the first rather than the second year. Other perceptions changed more during the second year than the first. For example, little change occurred in perceptions of the influence of the North-South conflict input during the first year (.10 points), but during the second year there was a substantial .80 point change.

Table 6.4 suggests a moderate relationship between veterans' perceptions and the period of time during which freshmen perceptions changed. Change which occurred largely in the first year was usually (64%) toward veterans' perceptions. On the other hand, change which occurred mainly in the second year appears to be more often (62%) away from veterans' perceptions. This pattern is perhaps best stated by noting that the association between the two variables was a moderate .489.

Some Stable Perceptions. Not too surprisingly, some perceptions were little changed by legislative experience. The most obvious example from our data is the perception of the influence of local community leaders. Given an initial influence score of 2.90, the change after one year was a −.03. After a second year, the perception score increased by .03 for a net change of zero after two years' legislative experience. The perceptions of the influence of the conflict between city and suburb exhibited a similar pattern. Clearly, these two perceptions remained essentially unchanged from their pre-legislative position.

The General Pattern. Overall, what was the impact of legislative service in the first term? The correlation between freshman per-

Table 6.4: Veterans' Perceptions and Time of Change in Freshmen's Perceptions

	Time of Greatest Change	
Trend:	First Year	Second Year
Toward Veterans	64%	38%
Away from Veterans	36%	62%
N:*	11	8
		G = .489

*In two cases, change occurred at approximately the same rate in each year.

ceptions prior to service and after two years was .845. Again, by use of the r^2 technique, we can reasonably suggest that after two years of legislative experience about seventy percent [$(.845)^2$ = .714] of the selected input perceptions were rooted in pre-legislative experience. Our hypothesis is not disproved by these findings, but it must be acknowledged at this point it appears that the preparatory legislative socialization phase is far more important in developing input perceptions than we had expected and, concomitantly, the impact of legislative service on these perceptions was not nearly as great.

Perceptual Consensus

Our second hypothesis was that legislative experience would produce greater agreement among freshmen. Table 6.5 presents our findings. Using the standard deviation as a measure of the range of perceptions, it was possible to measure the consensus changes which occurred during the first two years of legislative service. When the standard deviation for a particular perception becomes smaller over time, it suggests greater agreement or consensus. It is also possible, by comparing standard deviations, to see which perceptions freshmen were in most or least agreement about. Examining the first column (freshman perceptions prior to legislative service), we find the greatest agreement, for example, about the influence of the Speaker (S.D. = 0.81) and committees (S.D. = 0.82). On the other hand, there was least agreement about the influence of state political parties (S.D. = 1.65), and parliamentary procedure (S.D. = 1.63). If our second hypothesis is correct, we should find progressively smaller standard deviations for all or most of the input perceptions over time. As deviation decreases, agreement increases.

For example, the standard deviation—or range—of perceptions about the influence of the Speaker decreased between the first and second interview (from 0.81 to 0.51)—hence greater agreement. After another year's legislative experience, the range increased (to 0.70) but was still smaller than the original value (0.81). In this case, two years' legislative experience is associated with a decrease in range of perceptions about the influence of the Speaker. While the reduction is not linear, we can still say

Table 6.5: Ranges of Perceived Input Influence by Freshmen and Veteran Legislators

Input Factor	Panel Standard Deviations				Agreement Rankings			
	I	II	III	Vets	I	II	III	Vets
North v. South	1.61	1.67	1.28	1.20	19	20	14	8.5
Urban v. Rural	1.48	1.22	1.40	1.42	18	9.5	18	17
City v. Suburb	1.37	1.81	1.31	1.44	16	21	15.5	18
City Government	1.23	1.49	1.51	1.00	12	16	20	4
County Government	1.28	1.52	1.49	1.08	13	18	19	5
Local Business Leaders	1.17	1.03	0.92	1.22	10	5	4	11
Local Labor Leaders	1.22	1.41	1.16	1.22	11	15	10	11
Local Community Leaders	0.99	1.14	1.10	1.13	5	7	8	6
Local Political Leaders	1.01	1.22	0.91	1.28	6	9.5	3	13
State Political Parties	1.65	1.63	1.02	1.30	21	19	6	14
Minority Leader	1.32	1.38	1.31	1.20	15	13	15.5	8.5
Speaker	0.81	0.51	0.70	0.40	1	1	2	1
Committees	0.82	0.82	0.64	1.18	2	2	1	7
Committee Chairmen	0.90	0.85	0.96	0.92	3	3	5	3
Governor	1.41	1.17	1.21	1.22	17	8	11	11
State Bureaucracy	1.03	0.99	1.33	1.35	7	4	17	15.5
State Senate	1.10	1.33	1.22	2.01	9	11	12	21
Federal Government	1.06	1.39	1.65	1.35	8	14	21	15.5
Interest Groups	0.94	1.12	1.05	0.78	4	6	7	2
Parliamentary Procedure	1.63	1.51	1.27	1.81	20	17	13	20
Each Legislator's Own Ideology	1.29	1.34	1.25	1.59	14	12	9	19

generally that legislative experience is associated with a greater agreement or consensus in perceptions about the influence of the Speaker. Thus, the data in this case support our hypothesis.

Contrary to expectations, however, this pattern of increasing agreement was not always found for each of the twenty-one perceptions. Consensus about the influence of city government decreased—from a pre-legislative S.D. of 1.23 to 1.49 after one year's legislative experience—and continued with a further slight change to 1.51 after two years' experience. This pattern of decreasing consensus is in direct contradiction to our hypothesis. Moreover, this is not an isolated instance. In fact, no consistent pattern of increasing consensus associated with legislative experience is suggested in Table 6.5.

During the first year, of the nineteen perceptions exhibiting meaningful change in levels of agreement, twelve moved toward dissonance (63%). (We do not consider the change in state political parties from 1.65 to 1.63 to be meaningful; "committees" exhibited no change.) In the second year, of the seventeen perceptions showing meaningful change in levels of agreement, twelve moved toward consensus (71%). For the two-year period as a whole, there was a meaningful change in consensus for twenty of the twenty-one perception items (there was no appreciable change for "Minority Leader"). For twelve perceptions (60%), there was a trend toward consensus. Generally, the legislative experience of freshmen appears to have produced slightly more consensus than dissensus. But it was not until their second year that freshmen began to exhibit a slight pattern of increasing consensus.

Veteran Influence. A comparison of freshman consensus change with veteran consensus levels reveals very little association. For example, during the first year, freshman consensus about the influence of the Speaker increased, approaching the veteran's consensus (see Table 6.5). But, on the other hand, freshman consensus about the influence of city government decreased, moving away from that of the veterans. In none of the three time periods considered—first year, second year, or first term—were the associations between freshman consensus change and veteran consensus levels meaningful (see Table 6.6). The correlations were consistently low. Clearly, these data offer little support for the hypothesis that veterans are significant in the socialization process.

But perhaps the consensual changes which were negligible obscured the relationship for those that were substantial. In order to test for this, we have considered the direction of change by period of greatest change. For example, the level of consensus about the influence of committees did not change at all during the first year. But during the second year there was some change away from the level of consensus held by veterans. Is that significant?

The findings in Table 6.7 suggest no meaningful relationship be-

Table 6.6: Association Between Freshmen Consensus Change and Veterans'
Consensus Levels

Increased Freshman Consensus:	Direction of Freshman Consensus Change—Toward Veteran Levels	N
First Year	−.282	19
Second Year	−.200	17
First Term	−.167	20

Table 6.7: Period of Greatest Change in Freshman Consensus by Direction
of Change

| Direction of Change: | Period of Greatest Change In Consensus Levels | |
	First Year	Second Year
Toward Veterans	56%	50%
Away from Veterans	44%	50%
N:*	9	10
		G = .111

*N is less than 21 because the amount of change was essentially the same in both years
for two perceptions (local business leaders and minority leader).

tween the levels of consensus held by veterans and the changes in
freshman consensus. The negligible gamma (.111) does not provide
any reason to believe that veterans served as an important socializing factor in producing consensus about the influence of legislative inputs.

Our data suggest that the first year of legislative service tended
to produce slight dissonance among freshmen in regard to their
perceptions of legislative inputs while the second year tended to
produce slight consensus. For the two-year period as a whole,
there was a slightly greater tendency toward consensus than dissonance. But for none of the periods of time considered did
veterans appear to play a meaningful socializing role regarding
these particular input perceptions. In fact, using a Spearman rank
correlation technique, we find that the correlation between freshman and veteran levels of agreement decreased after two years.
Prior to legislative service, the correlation between freshmen-to-be
consensus and that of veterans was .493; after two years it was
reduced to .298. (Replication of the analysis presented earlier in
Table 6.3 revealed no meaningful association between veterans'
levels of agreement and the initial gap between freshmen's and
veterans' consensus. For that reason, it has not been presented
here.)

It is clear that there was neither a substantial increase in consensus among freshmen nor a substantial movement toward the
veteran consensual levels after two years of legislative experience.
In fact, the major impact of legislative service appears to have been
to substantially alter consensual levels in such a way that only one

discernible pattern emerges: there was only a moderate relationship between the initial levels of agreement and the levels two years later. This conclusion is supported by the fact that the correlation between initial consensual levels (prior to legislative service) and consensual levels after two years was .432. This suggests that little of the original consensual levels remained after legislative experience, and that most (about eighty percent) of the eventual consensus was a product of that experience. If this change was not one of increasing consensus (as we have seen), what could explain the process?

Polarization of Perceptions

Perhaps legislative service produces less, rather than more, consensus concerning the influence of certain legislative inputs. One possible explanation for this phenomenon is *polarization*. Polarization would tend to create two perceptual positions, creating disagreement rather than agreement. Three obvious potential polarizing factors are party, region, and ideology. For example, one might easily expect that legislators' perceptions about the influence of the state Senate would be associated with region; that perceptions about the influence of the federal government might be associated with ideology or that perceptions about the influence of city government might be associated with party. (Until the court-ordered reapportionment of 1965, state Senate seats were apportioned on a county basis and were, as a result, largely located in the rural and northern areas of the state.) Certainly, the fact that freshmen agreed less about these particular inputs after two years of legislative experience suggests something was pulling them apart. Thus, we hypothesized that dissonance was associated with polarization.

In order to test this hypothesis, correlations were calculated between freshman's party (Democrat and Republican) and influence scores; between region (North and South) and influence scores; and between ideology (liberal and conservative) and influence scores. Our findings are presented in Tables 6.8, 6.9, and 6.10. These tables present the correlations between input perceptions and the three suspected *polarizing factors* of party (Table 6.8), region (Table 6.9), and ideology (Table 6.10). Statistically, any

Table 6.8: Political Party as a Polarizing Factor

Input:	Correlation with Party*		
	Before Legislative Service	After One Year's Legislative Service	After Two Year's Legislative Service
CITY GOVERNMENT**	.002	−.572	−1.000
CITY V. SUBURB	.171	.482	.190
Local Political Leaders	.000	.342	.279
COUNTY GOVERNMENT	−.079	−.295	−.599
Speaker	−.173	−.294	.041
Committees	−.041	−.284	−.073
Local Labor Leaders	−.140	.280	.187
Urban v. Rural	.109	.250	.384
Federal Government	.092	−.191	−.167
State Senate	.000	.066	.061
Legislator's Own Ideology	.034	−.019	.130
North v. South	−.079	.046	.151
Committee Chairmen	.147	.083	−.291
Minority Leader	−.155	−.112	−.435
Interest Groups	.176	.036	.099
Bureaucracy	.201	−.180	.121
Parliamentary Procedure	.203	−.110	.129
Local Community Leaders	−.209	−.066	−.169
Political Parties	−.227	−.009	−.041
Governor Reagan	−.326	−.086	.349
Local Businessmen ***	−.432	−.245	−.183

*The "—" sign means that Republican freshmen see the input as more influential than do Democrats.

**Factors in capital letters are considered to have been meaningfully polarized during either, or both, the first or second year.

***Factors in italics are considered to have been appreciably de-polarized during the second year.

legislative input which correlated more strongly with one of the factors after legislative experience than before could be considered to have been polarized by that factor. However, for our purposes, in order to be considered *meaningfully polarized,* the correlation must not only have increased, but must have become at least ±.448. In this way, we can assert both that the perception became more strongly associated with the suspected polarizing factor, and that the polarizing factor accounted for at least twenty percent of the perception.

Party as a Polarizing Factor. Examination of Table 6.8 reveals that prior to legislative service, no perception was meaningfully associated with party.[5] (Local businessmen came close, however,

Table 6.9: Region as a Polarizing Factor

	Correlation with Region*		
Factor:	Before Legislative Service	After One Year's Legislative Service	After Two Year's Legislative Service
LOCAL COMMUNITY LEADERS**	.489	.752	.027
POLITICAL PARTIES***	.457	.521	.031
MINORITY LEADER	.222	.498	.330
Urban v. Rural	.190	.422	−.069
Committee Chairmen	−.145	−.332	−.325
Local Labor Leaders	.186	.311	.101
State Bureaucracy	−.124	−.301	−.338
Parliamentary Procedure	.169	.289	.128
City Government	−.031	.260	.274
North v. South	−.026	−.258	.136
Local Businessmen	.208	.244	−.057
Speaker	−.157	.242	−.107
STATE SENATE	−.202	.209	−.493
GOVERNOR REAGAN	.091	.051	−.515
City v. Suburb	−.209	.131	.108
Interest Groups	−.272	.016	−.044
County Government	−.340	.218	.128
Committees	−.407	.046	−.014
Local Political Leaders	.446	.420	−.193
Federal Government	−.510	.263	.027
Legislator's Own Ideology	.714	.462	−.319

*The "−" sign means that southern freshmen see the input as more influential than do northern.
**Factors in capital letters are considered to have been meaningfully polarized during either, or both, the first or second year.
***Factors in italics are considered to have been appreciably de-polarized during either, or both, the first or second year.

with a −.432). One year later, two perceptions met our criteria of change and strength, the influence of city government increased from .002 to −.572 and the correlation with perceptions of city versus suburb increased from .171 to .482. Thus, we can say that after one year's legislative experience, two perceptions were meaningfully polarized by party. During the second year, a third perception, county government, was meaningfully polarized from −.295 to −.599, while perceptions of the influence of city government were further polarized to a perfect −1.00. On the other hand, the perception of city versus suburb *depolarized* to .190. Thus, at the end of two years' service, only two freshman perceptions were meaningfully associated with party. (We might also

Table 6.10: Ideology as a Polarizing Factor

	Correlation with Ideology*		
Factor:	Before Legislative Service	After One Year's Legis- lative Service	After Two Year's Legis- lative Service
URBAN V. RURAL**	−.139	−.434	−.669
City v. Suburb	−.060	−.406	−.398
Local Political Parties	−.151	−.295	−.266
Local Labor Leaders	.070	−.267	−.221
Minority Leader	−.159	.235	.392
Political Parties	.052	−.214	.038
CITY GOVERNMENT	−.090	.150	.690
County Government	−.112	.138	.414
Parliamentary Procedure	.101	.109	.063
State Senate	−.064	−.094	.000
Speaker	−.055	−.063	−.142
Federal Government	−.003	.018	−.133
COMMITTEES	−.065	.060	.623
North v. South	−.126	.075	.204
Committee Chairmen	−.153	−.034	.238
Governor Reagan	.168	.022	.384
State Bureaucracy	−.237	.231	−.271
Interest Groups	−.256	−.230	−.079
Local Community Leaders	.293	.126	−.189
Each Legislator's Own Ideology	−.335	−.065	−.272
Local Businessmen	.365	.147	.193

*The "−" sign means that liberal freshmen see the input as more influential than do conservatives.
**Same as in Table 6.8.

note that the perception of the influence of the minority leader came close to meeting the criteria value.)

Region as a Polarizing Factor. A cursory reading of the three tables suggests that, of the three polarizing factors considered, region was the most important.[6] Most of this, however, stems from an initial polarizing effect *before legislative service.* Four perceptions substantially associated with region prior to legislative experience: local community leader's influence (.489), political parties' influence (.457), the federal government's influence (−.510), and the influence of the legislator's own ideology (.714). After one year, two of these perceptions were even more strongly associated with region: local community leaders (.752) and political parties (.521). In addition, freshman perceptions of the influence of the minority leader became polarized (.498). However, a reverse process was also at work; the perception of the influence of the federal government was depolarized (.263), while the polarization of the legislator's own ideology was markedly reduced (.462 compared to the previous .714). It was, however, the second year's legislative experience which eliminated region as the major polarizing factor. Only two perceptions were meaningfully associated with region after two years: governor's influence (−.515) and state Senate (−.493). Thus, what at first was an important polarizing factor was substantially reduced in significance after two years. These findings, of course, coincide with the findings in Tables 6.1 and 6.2, which showed a substantial drop in the perceived influence of the North-South split.

Ideology as a Polarizing Factor. A third possible source of perception polarization was ideology.[7] Our findings, presented in Table 6.10, suggest that ideology, like party and region, was not a very significant source of polarization. Initially, there was no meaningful association between ideology and perceptions. After the first year's legislative experience, two perceptions approached, but did not meet our minimal criterion values (urban versus rural and city versus suburb). After two years' legislative experience, three perceptions became substantially associated with ideology— urban versus rural (−.669), committees (.623), and city government (.690). One other perception approached the criterion value (county government). Thus, ideology which initially appeared to be of no consequence (following our first two series of interviews) became, by the end of the first term, the most significant of the three polarizing factors considered.

An Overview. During the first term, at one time or another, twelve of the input perceptions were polarized by party, region, or ideology. Prior to serving in the legislature, region was the only factor which polarized perceptions. At the end of the first term, party accounted for two polarizations, region accounted for two, and ideology accounted for three. (Since city government perceptions were polarized by both party and ideology, the total is six.) Thus, in general, polarization increased slightly during the first term. And ideology replaced region as the most significant polarizing factor (see Table 6.11).

But none of the factors considered polarized more than four perceptions, and nine of the perceptions (43%) were never polar-

Table 6.11: Summary of Polarized Perceptions*

| Polarizing Factor | Perceptions Polarized | | |
	Prior to Legislative Service	At End of First Year	At End of First Term
Party	none	City Government	City Government
		City v. Suburb	
			County Government
Region	Local Community Leaders	Local Community Leaders	
	Political Parties	Partical Parties	
	Legislators Own Ideology	Legislators Own Ideology	
			Governor
			State Senate
Ideology	none	none	Urban v. Rural
			Committees
			City Government

*Listing only those factor-perception correlations $\geq$.448.

ized. Further, none of the perceptions originally polarized remained so at the end of the first term. (Students of the legislative process might find it useful to consider the associations which existed between party, region and ideology and the perceptions of influence at the end of the first term [see the last column in Table 6.11]. These polarizations, if they continue, could be significant in the legislative process.)

This discussion began with the suggestion that the dissonance produced by legislative service might be the product of polarization. And, in fact, we found a slight majority of perceptions (57%) were polarized during some part of the time period examined (though none was consistently polarized). There is an indication in the foregoing data, then, of some association between dissonance and polarization. And, as expected, upon investigation we found a strong .765 association between polarization and dissonance. Table 6.12 categorizes each perception which was either polarized or depolarized, and indicates whether such a process was associated with increasing consensus or with dissonance.

Table 6.12: Polarization and Consensus Change Among Freshmen
Assemblymen

	Changes in Polarization*	
Changes in Consensus	Became Polarized	Became Depolarized
Decreasing Consensus (Dissonance)	43%	17%
No Change in Consensus**	43	0
Increasing Consensus	14	83
N:	7	6
	G = .765	

*Change which occurred during either the first or second year.
**A change ≤.05 points for the period of time under construction.

Summary

Freshmen Assembly members arrived at the state capitol with many perceptions about the influence of various legislative input factors. Some factors, like the Speaker and committees, were perceived as being quite influential; others, like the supposed conflict between city and suburb, or the role of local business leaders, were perceived as being of little influence in the legislative process.

Legislative experience substantially altered only a few perceptions. After one year's service, freshmen increased their assessment of the governor's influence and decreased their assessment of the federal government's. During the second year's experience, the assessment of the impact of state political parties and interest groups substantially increased. On the other hand, the traditional conflict between North and South was accorded much less importance.

Interestingly, newcomers' perceptions were not substantially different from veterans' (r_s = .650). Two years later, freshman perceptions were even more like veterans' (r_s = .809). Thus, it appears that legislative experience helped produce a greater agreement about perceptions of selected legislative inputs. On the other hand, the quite strong correlation of .845 between freshmen's pre-legislative perceptions and perceptions held two years later, argues that about seventy percent of freshman perceptions were a product of pre-legislative experience.

Further analysis suggests that freshman perceptions were more likely to move toward those of the veterans when the initial gap between freshman and veteran perceptions was greater than average. Examination of the time of greatest perceptual change (first-year or second-year) suggests that first-year changes were more likely to be toward those held by veterans. Thus, when veterans exercised some socializing influence, it was more likely to occur in the first, rather than in the second year, and in those cases where there was a substantial gap between veterans' and freshman perceptions.

We also attempted to assess the impact of legislative experience upon freshman perceptual consensus. Generally, legislative service appears to have produced only a little more consensus than dissonance. During the first year, change was more frequently toward dissonance, but in the second year some consensus was produced. However, unlike perceptions of influence, there was no apparent impact by veterans upon freshman consensus. Also, unlike perceptions of influence, the pre-legislative consensual patterns were only slightly like those found two years later. It appears that about eighty percent of consensus at the end of the first term was a product of legislative experience. These findings led us to look for some factors that might explain the unexpected pattern of dissonance.

We examined three factors usually considered to be significant in the polarization of legislative perceptions—party, region, and ideology. Prior to legislative service, party and ideology were not polarising factors. On the other hand, freshmen entered legislative service with four perceptions moderately influenced by region. During the entire two-year legislative period under examination, fifty-seven percent of freshmen's perceptions were at one time or another polarized by one of the three factors considered. On the other hand, almost half were never associated with these supposedly polarizing factors. And, by the end of two years' experience, only six perceptions (29%) were meaningfully polarized. While in overall terms, polarization was not as general a process as we anticipated, it did substantially correlate with dissonance when it occurred (G = .764).

In summary, our first hypothesis, that freshman perceptions would become more like those of veterans, was substantiated. But this was not due as much to legislative service as to pre-legislative experience. Perhaps the recruitment process is more vital than the socialization process. Our second hypothesis, that legislative service would produce greater perceptual consensus, did not prove out. In this case, perhaps forces external to the legislature were of greater significance.

While there was clearly a process of socialization taking place in the specific socialization phase, it is also equally clear that pre-legislative experience, or in our model terms, the preparatory legislative socialization phase, was considerably more important than we originally expected. Obviously, extrapolating general group theory to legislative bodies must be done with considerable caution. There is a substantial difference between the opinion/attitude dynamics within an artificially created group (e.g., Ash or Sherif) or of a group which exercises control over admission than there is in a legislature which has little control over admission to membership, which is structured in several ways for conflict, and which is anything but artificial.[8]

NOTES

1. Wahlke et al., op. cit.; Kenneth Prewitt et al., "Political Socialization and Political Roles," *Public Opinion Quarterly,* XXX (Winter 1966-1967); and Ronald D. Hedlund, "Legislative Socialization and Role Orientation," Report 11, Laboratory for Political Research, Department of Political Science, University of Iowa, October 1967.

2. Herbert McClosky, Paul J. Hoffman, and Rosemary O'Hara, "Issue Conflict and Consensus Among Party Leaders and Followers," *American Political Science Review,* LIV (June 1960), pp. 406-427. McClosky et al., found that political leaders in opposite parties disagreed more on issues than did rank-and-file members of the opposite parties.

3. In a relevant recent study of political organization, Edmond Constantini suggests that, in political organizations, those who are primarily concerned with issues tend to take more extreme positions than do those who are concerned with the winning of elections. Edmond Constantini, *The Democratic Leadership Corps in California* (Davis, Calif.: Institute of Governmental Affairs, 1967), p. 134.

4. For a discussion of gamma, or (as it is sometimes called) Goodman and Kruskal's coefficient of ordinal association, see Linton C. Freeman, *Elementary Applied Statistics* (New York: John Wiley, 1968).

5. The role of party in the legislative process is clearly different in the many states' legislatures. According to one recent study, about one-fifth of the state legislatures have strong party organization. See Belle Zeller, ed., *American State Legislatures* (New York: Thomas Y. Crowell, 1954), pp. 194-197. For a description of the relatively strong party caucus system in Connecticut's legislature, see Duane Lockhard, *New England State Politics* (Princeton: Princeton University Press, 1959), p. 218. On the other hand, California's legislature, like most, is not reputed to have strong party discipline. See William

Buchanan, *Legislative Partisanship* (Berkeley and Los Angeles: University of California Press, 1963). Also, see Frank J. Sorauf, *Party and Representation* (New York: Atherton Press, 1963).

6. Freshmen were assigned to the "southern" or "northern" region depending on whether their district was south or north of the Tehachapi Mountains. This has been a traditional dividing line in the state; many state agencies have their regional offices located on this basis and, perhaps most significantly, the line is used as a criterion for dividing highway construction funds. See Charles M. Price, "Classifying State Legislatures into Regional Groupings: The California Model," *Journalism Quarterly,* XLV (Summer 1968). For other research on the impact of regionalism, see Robert S. Friedman, "The Urban-Rural Conflict Revisited," *Western Political Quarterly,* XIV (June 1961), pp. 481-495; Dean E. McHenry, "Urban v. Rural in California," *National Municipal Review,* XXXV (July 1946), p. 350; or David R. Derge, "Metropolitan and Outstate Alignments in Illinois and Missouri Legislative Delegations," *American Political Science Review,* LII (December 1958). A reading of this and other literature suggests that, aside from reapportionment, the rural-urban conflict has been substantially reduced in state legislatures in recent years. However, our data suggest that freshmen saw it as being somewhat significant (ranked ninth in importance).

7. Freshmen were categorized as liberal or conservative on the basis of their responses to a nine-point self-anchoring ideology scale. Ideology was perceived by freshmen as a moderately influential legislative input. Of significance is the fact that it was ranked tenth compared to interest groups (sixth) and state political parties (ninth). After two years' service, these three "outside" or noninstitutional forces were perceived as more important than the other noninstitutional forces such as "North versus South," "local labor leaders," or the "federal government."

8. Muzafer Sherif, "Group Influences Upon the Formation of Norms and Attitudes," in *Readings in Social Psychology,* Theodore M. Newcomb and Eugene L. Hartley, eds. (New York: Henry Holt, 1947), pp. 77-90; and Solomon E. Ash, "Effects of Group Pressure Upon Modification and Distortion of Judgments," *Group Dynamics,* op. cit., pp. 189-200.

Chapter 7

SUMMARY AND CONCLUSIONS

In this chapter we shall attempt to incorporate into our phase-process model of legislative socialization (described in Chapter 2) the findings reported in Chapters 3-6. Our model includes four reasonably distinct time-span socialization phases and four types of socializing processes—the main components of which are presented in Figure 7.1.

Phases

The preparatory legislative socialization phase can be considered the "before" stage of legislative socialization, including all of the pre-legislative life experiences that bear upon the individual's later career as legislator. Within this phase there are two periods. "Basic" socialization is the period of time from early childhood when a citizen's primary political attitudes are formed. "Transitional" socialization is a time of heightened political activity which, for the class of '66, certainly began no later than the point when each made the decision to run for political office.

The specific socialization phase, or the "after" phase, includes the relevant experiences shaping and influencing the new legislator

Process:	Phases			
	Preparatory Legislative Socialization Phase		Specific Legislative Socialization Phase	
	Basic Socialization Period	Transitional Socialization Period	Initial Legislative Socialization Period	Secondary Legislative Socialization Period
Accumulation				
Interpersonal				
Identification				
Cognitive-Developmental				

Figure 7.1: A PHASE-PROCESS MODEL OF LEGISLATIVE SOCIALIZATION

after assuming office. "Initial legislative" socialization is that period of one's legislative career when (s)he is a newcomer, or a freshmen legislator. "Secondary legislative" socialization is the period when a legislator moves in one of three directions:

(1) gains acceptance and respect from colleagues and, depending to some extent on his or her party affiliation, gets selected or elected to a party leadership position, committee chairmanship, or powerful committee:

(2) gets along reasonably well with colleagues but for various reasons—indifference, lack of ambition, personality quirks, lack of intelligence or whatever—fails to gain the necessary sort of respect and confidence from colleagues to propel him or her into a leadership position; and

(3) refuses to go along with the niceties of the legislature, is not liked by colleagues and never elected or selected to a position of influence.

Certainly it is recognized that these periods may overlap, and the dividing line separating one period from another is not always precise. For example, when does a person reach the transitional socialization period—after working in one campaign, or several, or contributing money to a candidate, or serving on a school board? Admittedly, the determination of whether an individual has reached the transitional phase is arbitrary. However, we would argue that the decision *to run* for political office *definitely* marks a sharp departure from the basic socialization phase and is symptomatic of an unusual and heightened political socialization. Similarly, does initial legislative socialization commence after getting elected, or does it begin after going to the state capitol and being officially sworn in? In California, the new legislator finds him- or herself intensely involved in several aspects of legislative political life immediately upon election in early November.[1] On the other hand, he or she is not an official lawmaker until December (Proposition 4, passed by the voters in November 1972, moved the first day of the new term to early December of even numbered years.) Or when does a legislator reach the secondary legislative socialization period—after a few months, the first year, several years, or many years? Though there are difficulties such as these in delineating the periods, we feel it useful, nevertheless, when considering legislative socialization, to view it as a relatively segmented continuum.

Process

In order to better understand not only the sequence of events but also the process involved, we have grafted onto our period-phase model described above the process model developed by Robert Hess and Judith Torney. In their study of children's political socialization, they present four process models.

> Four models (accumulation, interpersonal, identification, and cognitive-developmental) are suggested which describe in different ways the acquisition, change, and stabilization of political attitudes. These are not formal explanatory models but devices for examining the attitudes the child brings to the socialization process and the way he utilizes experience in the development of political roles.[2]

Our initial theoretical framework was structured around the time periods previously discussed. However, because we were greatly impressed with the political socialization models used by Hess and Torney and found them both attractive and inventive, we decided to attempt to apply them to our data. Briefly, their four processes or models can be described in the following way.[3] "Accumulation"—in this model, the development of role expectations proceeds through one's acquisition of specific units of knowledge, information, attitudes, and activities. "Interpersonal transfer"—in this model, the experiences in interpersonal relationships, the ways of doing things, and attitudes toward authority figures may be transferred to one's relationships in the legislature. "Identification"—in this model, one imitates the behavior of a significant person. This transmission is inadvertent, though some politicians may consciously pattern themselves after an admired or successful political figure. "Cognitive-developmental"—in this model, the ability to deal with concepts or information sets limits on one's understanding of the socialization process.

The Hess and Torney socialization models were developed to study children. It was our feeling, however, that research on socialization could proceed more meaningfully and data compared more successfully if common theoretical constructs could be used. A major difficulty in using these process models in our study was that Hess and Torney focus primarily on the political socialization and development of political attitudes of a cross-section of American children; our study focuses on the socialization of a select adult elite.

For these reasons, the reader should keep in mind the model's imperfections when we attempt to apply in the following pages the Hess and Torney processes of accumulation, interpersonal, identification, and cognitive-developmental to our own study. It should be noted too, that, like Hess and Torney in their study of the political socialization of children, we found that particular socialization models could be applied better in some periods than in others; thus not every cell in Figure 7.2 is filled. Our attempt here is to be illustrative rather than comprehensive. However, we are convinced that these models do provide an important theoretical dimension to our study. But because of the problems of applying the Hess and Torney models, and also because of the environmental and methodological limits of the study, the generalizations and commentary of the following sections must be considered preliminary.

Period 1: Basic Political Socialization

No other aspect of socialization has been studied so extensively as the child's acquisition of politically relevant attitudes, values, norms, and perceptions—his or her political development as a citizen. There is no need here to retrace that familiar terrain. Moreover, the main thrust of this study is directed toward the adult years and, in particular, a select segment of adults. However, for purposes of symmetry, a few remarks about each process in this period are in order.

ACCUMULATION

Basic political socialization of the thirty-three members of the class of '66 appears to have proceeded in much the same way as for most Americans—families, schools, churches, peer, and later occupational groups acted as socializing agencies in citizenship development and political attitude formation.[4] A basic knowledge and understanding of our system of government through specific units of information were passed on to these newcomers through a process that Hess and Torney describe as accumulation. There is some evidence, however, to suggest that this basic political socialization was more intense and occurred somewhat earlier for our respondents than for the typical citizen.[5]

Members of the class of '66 were typical of the adult population of the state in some respects. However, in several respects, class members were quite unlike the adult population of the state—first, the predominance of males; and second, the greater educational achievement and generally higher social status of the members. These unique features of the class coincide with the socialization findings of Hess and Torney: (1) "boys consistently display more active involvement and politicized concern than girls; and (2) the acquisition and initiatory aspects of political involvement (activities, participation in discussion, interest) is strongly affected by IQ and by social status."[6] Moreover, children with high intelligence coming from high-status homes are more likely to have a greater sense of political efficacy.[7] Political socialization was undoubtedly also facilitated by the years these legislative newcomers had spent in school. Though there is persuasive evidence that the typical school curriculum has almost no influence on political socialization per se, the general college and graduate school peer milieu probably reinforced political values and attitudes and helped develop traditional political skills.[8]

In terms of role development, our evidence suggests that the legislator's concept of the ideal representative role (i.e., delegate, politico, or trustee) was substantially formed during his pre-legislative life experiences. Further, on the basis of admittedly inferential data, we feel at this time that the initial representational role orientations were probably developed during period 1 rather than in period 2. A survey of 1,013 voters registered in California in May 1968 revealed that their preference for legislators' representational roles was quite similar to the roles initially chosen by our freshmen-to-be. (Data were collected by the California Poll under contract with the authors. Respondents were given the same items used in the survey of legislators-to-be.)

Representative Role Orientations

Role:	California Registered Voters	Freshmen-to-be
Trustee	10%	10%
Politico	51	62
Delegate	39	28

We assume that, since most citizens never enter into period 2 socialization, their role preferences are developed in period 1. Thus, by inference, we have chosen to identify legislators' pre-legislative representative role orientations as also having been substantially developed during period 1.

INTERPERSONAL TRANSFER

The thirty-three freshmen came to the legislature with considerable experience in playing the role of newcomer. Certainly within the family the child must learn his or her "place," and if the family moves to a new residence, there is the age-old problem of socialization in being "the new kid on the block." There are the other inevitable growing-up problems of graduating to new classes and moving on to junior high, high school, and college that were experienced by all of our legislators. Later in life there are the problems of assimilation in the service, at work, in the neighborhood, and in community groups. Certainly, learning to play the role of newcomer in other organizations and situations would help develop skills and perceptions that could be transferred to the legislature.

Perhaps the best illustration of this model involves the rules of the game. Could not the sort of informal ways of doing things, or ways of acting learned in pre-legislative life, be applied in the legislative arena? Admittedly, for some, knowledge of the informal rules (i.e., former legislative staff employees) had come through a process of first-hand experience, and specific information passed on to them by various authority figures (accumulation), but this was not the case for most of the freshmen. As noted previously, most of legislative aspirants (23 or 74%) knew that there were informal rules operating in the legislature and could explain something about them. In the following pages within the various socialization phases and processes, we shall return to this material.

IDENTIFICATION

It is difficult to say with assurance that any of our freshman legislators consciously patterned their lives on the model of their parents, teachers, clergy, mayors, or some nationally prominent politicians, and it would have been necessary to probe deeply into the underlying psychological areas of our respondents' minds to be able to discern the unconscious. (Such a probe would have consumed too much of our restricted interview time.)

Several, but not many, of the new legislators had relatives or parents who had been elected officials, or who had been heavily involved in party activities. It is possible that these people could have served as models for the new legislator. Several of the freshmen suggested that they had first become active in politics because of the charisma of some nationally prominent politician such as Adlai Stevenson, Dwight D. Eisenhower, or John F. Kennedy. On the whole, however, probably few freshmen overtly patterned their behavior after one particular political figure. A composite of admired characteristics appears to be more the case.

COGNITIVE-DEVELOPMENTAL

The fact that our respondents were elected to the legislature argues that the cognitive-developmental limits of each were not sufficient to preclude the socialization required to get to period 2. Thus our data are not adequate to examine this process in period 1.

By implication, however, we can reasonably assume that each had the intelligence and energy to make it through the basic socialization period.

Period 2: Transitional Socialization

As noted previously, there is no precise dividing line separating basic political socialization from transitional socialization; the latter period is marked by heightened political activity—such as party work, community involvement, or political club endeavors. Of course, the clearest indication that an individual has reached the transitional socialization phase is the decision to file for political office. (Less than two percent of American citizens ever run for political office.)[9] Most members of the class of '66 were involved in local politics and were keenly aware of the impact that the 1965 reapportionment would have on the state legislative races—a dearth of incumbents with the concomitant opportunity for newcomers. Therefore, most legislative aspirants' decisions to run were not quixotic or spur-of-the-moment; these candidates had given careful thought to their chances and perceived the opportunity. It is true that in almost every election there are a *few* individuals who actually are "drafted" into running in particular districts—perhaps someone who has very little previous political experience.[10] However, almost without exception, those who are "drafted"—individuals who are urged to run by party or community leaders—are urged to do so because they have become well known in the community in nonpartisan capacities such as county president of the farm bureau, member of the city council, or county school superintendent. Thus, they almost inevitably must have developed some feel for the political process.

For many, the state legislature was a step up the political ladder. There is no rigid hierarchy of political office in California which dictates that a candidate must first run for lower office and then move on to run for higher office. But a good portion of the class of '66 had served previously at the local level—on school boards, city councils, or boards of supervisors and were now graduating upward. Thus, while we have defined the second period of political socialization as starting *no later* than with the decision to run, it is obvious that for most of our respondents, the second period had begun much earlier.

In his highly provocative and thoughtful comments on the adaptation of Connecticut freshmen lawmakers to the legislature, James Barber contends that filing for office marks a dramatic and sharp disruption in the occupational careers of legislative candidates.

> Furthermore, if there is a typical course it is to move from an occupational role one has held for years over into a political role. Unlike the relatively uncommitted new graduate in law or business, the new politician enters late upon a political career by breaking off (or severely bending) his connections with a regular, recognized occupational role and status. This decision represents an interruption or diversion from a relatively long-standing *personal* identity which the individual has established in his work. In a sense his candidacy is a public admission that there was something incomplete or unsatisfactory about the course he was pursuing.[11]

One would assume that the decision to run for the state legislature in California should be even more disruptive than in Connecticut, since the legislative position is so clearly full-time in the former. Undoubtedly, Barber's remarks describe the situation for some of our freshmen, but certainly not all. For example, five of the freshmen in the class of '66 were retired. Running for political office meant no disruption of their basic life careers because those were completed. Indeed, for retired persons in good health with considerable time opportunities, here was a chance to extend one's useful life. For the three former legislative staff employees who had already become partly socialized in the state capitol milieu, running in an "open" district was a golden opportunity, and the next logical step up the political ladder. For attorneys (fourteen), the decision to run for political office appears to be almost as natural and inevitable as taking on a new case. In addition to the advantages accruing to one's law firm, there was also the chance to move up in one's field due to the corollary potential opportunities for appointment to a judicial position, or perhaps eventual election as state attorney general.[12] Furthermore, legislator-lawyers can continue to practice law, though on a greatly reduced basis, while serving as legislators. Consequently, we would contend that, for at least two-thirds of the legislative newcomers in California, the decision to run for the state legislature was not so much an escape from an incomplete or unsatisfactory first occupation but a natural progression.

ACCUMULATION

Planning, organizing, and managing a political campaign take considerable skill and ingenuity, and the final responsibility for the effort usually rests with the individual candidate. However, nearly all of the thirty-three freshmen-to-be were considered "possible winners," and this meant that party leaders in the Assembly as well as other state party officials and interest groups were keenly concerned with the outcome of these races. Depending on a host of variables, such as party registration figures, strength of the candidate in the district, strength of his opposition, previous track record, ability to raise money, etc., considerable aid and assistance were given the new candidates. Schools for party candidates were established in different parts of the state. Candidates were invited to Sacramento to meet and confer with party officials and discuss how their campaigns were going. Caucus staff were "lent" to provide assistance in the campaign, and in some cases Democrats received help from department and agency staff. In a few instances, too, particularly on the Republican side, corporations lent staff to candidates. Incumbent legislators of the same party, usually from the same general area, could offer keen insights into the campaign strategies that might be employed. In short, learning about how to campaign fits the accumulation model—i.e., direct units of knowledge were acquired by the freshmen-to-be from veteran legislators, at candidates' schools, at party meetings at the district and state levels, and from staff personnel.

There is also evidence to suggest that the thirty-three freshmen-to-be had in their basic political socialization and transitional socialization periods become reasonably well informed about the legislative milieu. As noted in Chapter 6, there was a strong similarity between freshmen-to-be and veterans in perceptions of the importance of various legislative inputs ($r_s = .650$). Initially, the class of '66 perceived the Speaker, committee chairmen, committees, and the state Senate to be the most important factors in the legislative process, while constituent pressures such as local labor leaders, local community leaders, local political leaders, and local businessmen, along with the demands of city government and the issue of "city versus suburb" were rated as far less important factors in the legislative process. Even more significantly, the association between initial perceptions and those held after two years' legislative experience was quite strong (r_s = .845). Thus, about seventy percent of the sophomores' perceptions were rooted in the preparatory legislative socialization. Certainly, it would seem that the acquisition of perceptions of legislative input factors is a good example of the accumulation model. On the other hand, little of the original consensus remained after two years' experience in the Assembly. Finally, while neither party nor ideology had much impact on initial perceptions, region did polarize four perceptions (19%) prior to legislative experience.

As we saw in Chapter 5, the legislator's initial party and interest-group roles (unlike the representative roles) were substantially altered by legislative experience. There was no meaningful association between roles after two years' legislative service and prior to service. While it is tempting to suggest that these two roles, like the representative role, probably developed initially during period 1 (an argument by analogy), we are not willing to do so. And, though the argument for their having developed *initially* during period 2 is not much stronger, we feel that at present it is the better one. We suspect that the lack of stability in party and interest-group roles is rooted in their having been developed during period 2.

After the candidate's successful election effort, the legislator-to-be was immediately plunged into a whirl of pre-session activities. Undoubtedly, the most important events for the assemblyman-elect were the pre-session party caucuses. Along with discussions of political strategy and policy problems of the forthcoming session, there was the crucial vote to select the party leaders, particularly if one's party was in the majority and was, in effect, electing the Speaker. The legislator-to-be began to learn the rewards and penalties for supporting particular party leadership candidates. If the freshman voted for the "wrong" candidate (i.e., the losing Speaker candidate) he or she might have found upon arrival in Sacramento that the committees assignments requested were not available, or learned later that the bills he or she carried had great difficulty clearing committees. Thus, the several months leading up to the session were filled with advice, requests, and pressures from any number of different sources: senior legislators, lobbyists (including Operation Viewpoint), party people, and prominent and not so prominent constituents.

INTERPERSONAL TRANSFER

Our findings in Chapter 4 revealed that legislators-to-be often had a reasonably good understanding of the interpersonal rules of the legislature before being sworn-in. The data suggest that such knowledge was partially the result of political activity and partially associated with party and ideology. On the other hand, level of education, training in law, and community activity did not seem to be associated with rule sophistication. These latter findings suggest that rule sophistication was acquired in period 1—as a part of childhood education in good manners. The political correlates suggest period 2. On balance, we suggest that while courtesy and integrity are best learned in childhood, the political aspects (the *legislative* rules of the game) are more likely learned in a political (adult) milieu.

In addition, the skills, perceptions, and values of one's occupation and community concerns will be a factor in the initial committee assignments secured by freshmen during their first session (we discuss this point more fully later).

Several illustrations can also be proposed in regard to campaigns. Many political, social, and occupational skills possessed by the Assembly candidates could be easily transferred to the ordeals of a political campaign. Lawyers and school teachers as part of their jobs must learn how to speak in front of large audiences, field questions, and talk off the cuff—invaluable skills all political candidates should possess. In addition, lawyers represent clients in much the same way that legislators represent constituents. Or, as another example, the managerial and organizational skills that are the stock in trade of a businessman could easily be put to use running a political campaign, particularly in raising money, organizing precinct drives, or advertising in the local newspaper or on local radio or television. Thus, the skills that allow a school administrator to placate an angry parent, a lawyer to convince a jury, a teacher to interest a class, or a realtor to promote a sale are also features which might be transferred to the legislative arena. (Certainly, the mushrooming growth of public relations firms in political campaigns is a shining example of the transfer principle—from selling products to selling candidates.[13]

IDENTIFICATION

Several examples come to mind in suggesting how the identification model could apply to the transitional socialization period. First, we have already mentioned the rather extensive political campaign background experience of our respondents. Undoubtedly, these freshmen could have imitated candidates they had been most impressed with, or used parents and relatives who had been active politicians as models for their own candidacy. Second, as noted previously, several freshmen stated they had become involved in politics during the campaigns of Dwight Eisenhower, John F. Kennedy, and Adlai Stevenson. It could be suggested that among the attributes these three luminaries possessed as political candidates were: eloquence, wit, charm, and sincerity. It was our impression that some of our freshmen-to-be consciously or unconsciously imitated the "style" of one of these politicians.[14]

COGNITIVE-DEVELOPMENTAL

In a sense, the election victories scored by the freshmen members of the class of '66 suggest that they had at least sufficient energy, intelligence, and personality to get elected. Or, conversely, we can generally assume that any candidate *seriously lacking* in one of these qualities would likely have been weeded out in the primary election or certainly by the general election. Occasionally, perhaps, in California, in a safe district, it might be possible to elect someone who was deficient in some of these qualities. Moreover, it should be emphasized that we are referring to *minimal* requirements. With few exceptions, the freshmen, regardless of ideology or party affiliation, were energetic, bright, and friendly.

Period 3: Initial Legislative Socialization

In examining the socialization patterns of periods 1 and 2, we treated certain kinds of learning as a *transfer* process. That is, what was learned at one time and place was transferable to another time and place. However, in period 3 (and 4) what is learned is likely to be *immediately applied*. For example, learning the rules of the game, examined under the interpersonal transfer process model during periods 1 and 2 could easily be considered as later applicable in periods 3 and 4. But what is learned in period 3 is immediately applicable. Thus, in a narrow sense, since we are concerned with legislative socialization, what is learned after being sworn in is more likely to be immediately applicable. However, in the larger sense, as a study of socialization per se, almost any learning may be considered latently transferable to some future situation.

After the oath of office was administered in early January of 1967,[15] the thirty-three legislative aspirants became official California State Assembly members.[16] At that point they certainly entered period 3—initial legislative socialization.

The first weeks of the legislative session were perhaps the least hectic and frantic for the newcomers because committees had generally not begun meeting (not even organized). Moreover, there was a thirty-day lull between the time when bills are introduced and assigned to committee, and when they are heard. (The voters in 1972 abolished such recess situations, and the California legislature functions essentially for a two-year period.) However, even this early period is a busy one for state legislators, since a host of decisions must be made, and the "off" hours are particularly hectic, with new legislators receiving countless invitations to parties, receptions, banquets, and cocktail parties. There are two general realms in which crucial decisions must be made by the legislator: personal and legislative, and in both instances the accumulation model applies.

In the personal realm, one of the first considerations to be made by the new legislator is the decision whether or not to bring the family to Sacramento. Moving to Sacramento means enduring the expenses of a second home, transferring children in and out of school, placating wives who would have to leave friends and associates back at home or husbands who would have to leave jobs or commute, living far away from a "city" (such as Los Angeles, San Francisco, or San Diego) and, consequently, not getting back to the district as often as one should.[17] However, the advantage of moving is not being away from one's family four days out of every week.[18] As the job of legislator has become increasingly full-time, and as the new legislator becomes more secure in his or her position (particularly after getting reelected once), many legislators with families eventually move them to Sacramento.[19]

Another important personal decision for the new legislator involves his or her former occupation. Most freshmen legislators (except those who have already retired) attempt to remain at least minimally involved in their former occupations. Hence, part of Fridays and Saturdays back in the home constituency has to be devoted to putting in time at the law office or at the business in order to try to share some of the load that partners have assumed. However, as the years go by, and as the new legislator becomes a more vital cog in the Assembly, and as political opportunities and obligations increase, it seems that many California state legislators forego part-time work in their former occupations in order to concentrate solely on their legislative chores. Legislating becomes their only job.[20]

Personal decisions were made by legislators on these matters on the basis of their own views, those of their families, friends, work associates, *and* veteran legislators who had gone through the same problems.[21] PALS, the Protective Association of Lost Souls, has been sort of a legislators' wives sorority, which is open for all spouses to join. (PALS might well fall victim to the slowly growing number of women legislators, unless their husbands also join.) While it does perform charitable endeavors, a main function of the group is easing the transition from private life to public life in Sacramento. And, it seems almost inevitable that the newcomers in the legislature would turn to senior legislators whom they respected and ask for advice on these personal questions—a process of accumulation.

In the legislative realm, there were a number of initial problems for the freshmen: selecting a secretary, choosing an administrative assistant, selecting an office in the capitol building (the Assembly Rules Committee staff allows members to choose their office suites on the basis of seniority), setting up the district office, picking a state car, and—most important—attempting to get selected to committees in which they were most interested. These legislative decisions ranged in importance from the trivial and routine—i.e., selecting office quarters and automobiles—to more important choices such as selecting secretaries and administrative assistants and setting up the district office, to the most important decision—getting selected to the "right" committees.

Traditional advice given to most new legislators is to select secretaries who are familiar with the state capitol and who know "the ropes." Senior legislators frequently recommend particular secretaries to freshmen legislators. Some administrative assistants are selected because of their help in the campaign, because they have good ties in the home district, because they are friends of the legislator, or because they are recommended to the legislator by colleagues. Obviously, a crucial determinant in whether a local person or a Sacramento professional is picked is the role of the administrative assistant. Some legislators have their administrative assistants serve back home; other assistants remain in the legislator's Sacramento office. If the former role is desired by the legislator, a local assistant would probably be selected; if the latter, a Sacramento professional is the likelier choice.

Strategy followed by a freshman in getting preferred committee positions hinged around: (1) whether their party was in the majority and therefore had selected the Speaker; and if so (2) whether he or she had supported the Speaker in the pre-session party caucus. Many, probably most, freshmen have very little knowledge about the policy areas of each committee. And, often, the number of committees and areas of concern are changed at the beginning of a session. Freshmen are seldom selected to the most important committees (i.e., Rules Committee or Ways and Means Committee), nor are they given chairmanships. On the other hand, they usually get some committee assignments that they have requested. In seeking useful or interesting committee assignments, the freshmen class of '66 often turned to more senior Assembly members and then staff for advice: party and regional ties were important, and, of course, asking the Speaker directly often helped.

In addition, new legislators had to learn quickly about handling lobbyists, the mechanics of bill passage, how legislation is drafted, how to conduct oneself in committee and on the floor—in short, the overall role of a legislator. On these matters, the Rules Committee, veteran legislators, party caucuses, informal legislative groups, and the legislative staff—particularly the legislative council—provided help.

One of the most remarkable features of the California Assembly is the degree to which newcomers are allowed to take part in deliberations. From the outset, new members can speak up in committee hearings, introduce legislation, and participate in caucuses.[22] However, as with any group, the new freshmen in the Assembly were restricted in some ways. Freshmen did not carry many of the significant bills of the session, chaired none of the standing committees (except for one minor one); and with only one exception, they were not selected to serve on either the Ways and Means Committee or the Rules Committee, and were not elected to major party leadership positions. Freshmen were expected to be *somewhat* more reticent than their veteran colleagues and at times some senior members seemed to resent newcomers speaking up too quickly and at too much length on the floor, in committee, or in party caucus on matters about which they felt freshmen had only limited knowledge.[23] However, the restraints freshmen operated under in the Assembly were minimal; those with special expertise could participate immediately, and those with ability moved up swiftly. In learning the proper role of a freshman in the state legislature, individual veteran legislators, staff, informal groups, caucuses, and the like all imparted information to the new members.

ACCUMULATION

One of the first things that legislators learn in developing their role orientation is their relationship with "significant others." In terms of the role types that we examined—i.e., representative, interest group, and party—only the representative role was substantially rooted in pre-legislative life experiences. Interest-group role and party role were shaped almost exclusively by the legislative experience. Prior to serving in the legislature, most legislators-to-be tended to take middle-range role orientations i.e., politico for the representative role; neutral for the interest-group role; and nonpartisan for the party role. And, as discussed in

Chapter 5, there was a considerable amount of uncertainty and inconsistency in the role stance of the typical legislator both prior to service and during his or her first term in the legislature. About half the legislator's representational role was rooted in pre-legislative experience, while approximately twenty-five percent appears to have been the product of period 3.

Almost all of the Assemblyperson's interest-group role was the product of legislative experience. During this first year, it appears that about a third of the interest-group role was acquired. There is good reason to believe that micemilk helped shape and influence some legislators' interest-group role orientations, as did the day-to-day contact with legislators, reporters, and lobbyists themselves.[24] Party roles, too, were essentially the product of legislative experience. Almost half the freshman's party role appears to have been the product of this first session. Party role orientations were partially shaped by the two caucuses and by other informal groups such as the ghetto discussion group, the Black caucus, Bear's bunch, the conservative caucus, the party leadership of the two houses, individual members, and state party officials.

As noted previously, in Chapter 6, freshmen arrived at the state capitol with a number of perceptions about the relative importance of a variety of legislative input factors. For example, they perceived the Speaker, committees, committee chairmen, and the state Senate as being among the most influential legislative input factors. Conversely, they viewed city government and local community leaders as far less significant factors. While there were no great changes overall, a few perceptions did change markedly. Freshmen learned to appreciate the importance of the governor in the legislative process. On the other hand, their perceptions of the importance of the federal government dropped sharply.

The "learning" experience of legislative service did not always produce agreement. As we saw in Chapter 6, for a majority of input perceptions, there was less agreement after a year's legislative experience than there had been prior to being sworn-in! This, of course, does not suggest that legislators were not socialized by serving in the legislature, but that, rather, they were confronted by different kinds of experiences and responded to them in different ways. Some of the differences had to do with the "non-legislative" influences of party, region, and ideology. These they brought to the legislature, but these played a part in their activities as legislators and could be expected to exercise some influence on the perceptions of the input factors which we examined.

Of the three polarizing factors considered, two (party and region) had some impact. While party had not been associated with any perceptions before the first session, it was associated with two perceptions at the end of the first year. Region continued to influence four perceptions. Ideology remained, however, nonoperative.

Veterans also played something of a socializing role during this third period. There was a clear tendency among the freshmen to change their perceptions toward those of the veterans when there was a substantial difference between the two groups at the outset.

Nearly all the freshmen received at least one of their committee choices, and some were given virtually all they requested.[25] Committee assignments were often made on the basis of relevant background experience or information freshmen had acquired in their prior educational, political, occupational, and social lives. Thus, former teachers, school administrators, and school board members in the class of '66 were placed on the education committee; ranchers and farmers on the agriculture committee; lawyers on the judiciary and criminal procedures committee; businessmen on the industrial relations committee; lawyers and businessmen on the revenue and taxation committee; a dental technician and pharmacist on the public health committee; Black legislators on the social welfare committee; those from urban areas on the committee dealing with mass transit; and so on. In short, the knowledge these freshmen had acquired in their previous careers could be transferred to their committee work.

INTERPERSONAL TRANSFER

Freshmen began period 3 with substantially differing levels of knowledge about the rules of the game. (The following should be considered in light of our opening comments discussing period 3.) Some arrived with a rather more sophisticated grasp of the interpersonal rules of the game, while others had essentially no knowledge of them. With the exception of one freshman, none had a grasp of the legislative rules—how one behaves in specific committee situations, relations with lobbyists, party rules, etc. But, by the end of the first year, all the freshmen appeared to have gained a good grasp of the rules—interpersonal and legislative. Period 3 was the period in which all learned the specific legislative rules; and those who arrived ignorant of the interpersonal rules quickly caught up with their peers.

Thus, we could discern almost no differences among the members of the class of '66, with regard to their understanding of the rules of the game, after they had spent a year in the legislature. The swiftness and ease with which the rules were learned suggests a carryover from previous life experiences, as well as the efficacy of veteran legislators and others in advising the newcomers (accumulation). As we previously suggested, it would also seem likely that most freshmen had had considerable experience in their pre-legislative lives playing the role of newcomer and in learning how to get along with others and that these skills could have been transferred to the legislature.

IDENTIFICATION

It was our feeling that the newcomers did look to particular senior legislators as models for behavior. Frequently, too, in the course of our interviews, we could sense that Freshman A had been deeply influenced by Legislator X, and, repeatedly, certain veterans were referred to by freshmen as being helpful, able, or effective legislators. However, the identification process is difficult to assess with such a sophisticated sample, and our comments here are admittedly brief and speculative.

COGNITIVE-DEVELOPMENTAL

Every member of the class of '66 shared many of the same socializing experiences. All had had the same formal orientation by the Assembly Rules Committee and the Assembly Office of Research; all had undergone the same informal orientation with veteran legislators, Operation Viewpoint, the party caucuses, and the like. (In 1973, California freshmen were given a rigorous five-day orientation, co-sponsored by the Legislative Joint Rules Committee and the American Political Science Association [including the two authors as State Legislative Service Fellows].) Moreover, the class of '66 had roughly equivalent educational qualifications and came from similar social backgrounds. In the last analysis, they were all electable; that is, they had enough personality, dedication, and ability to be selected by the voters in a primary and a final election. Yet while there was this basic equivalency among class members, some quickly gained attention among their colleagues as "comers," while others never attained much recognition and were never seriously considered as Assembly leadership material. How do we account for these differences? Or, to phrase it more accurately, why were some freshman legislators considered highly effective, while others were not?

Part of the answer to legislative effectiveness, it seems would simply be willingness to work hard. (Good health is certainly an essential attribute.) Most freshmen worked very hard and put in extremely long hours, but some appeared to work harder than others. For those unfettered by family obligations, of course, it was easier to devote evenings and weekends to socializing with Assembly friends, studying and drafting bills, preparing for the next day's committee hearings, checking with colleagues on upcoming votes, or giving speeches at testimonial dinners, and the like. By participating extensively in all aspects of the legislative process, the new member could begin to develop a recognition among his colleagues. Another dimension of the work was whether the legislator genuinely enjoyed what he or she was doing. It was our impression that the hardest workers loved the job, enjoyed the excitement and glamour of being a legislator, were keenly concerned about getting reelected, and thought about further steps up the political ladder. A few freshman legislators tended to view legislative service as more of a duty, an obligation, or a crusade. They simply did not seem to have the same zest for the job that their peers had, and they did not move up the political ladder as rapidly.

Simply working hard, of course, is not sufficient for getting ahead in the legislature. Intelligence, personability, and flexibility were the attributes which appear to have contributed most to the overall effectiveness of the legislator. From our vantage, too, it would seem that overwhelming strength on one of these items could not completely compensate for weakness in another of the qualities. Thus, Legislator X might be extremely bright, and very knowledgeable about a particular subject of legislation. He or she might be able to explain to colleagues in very lucid terms the complexity of the topic and its ramifications. Yet, if unable to get along socially with colleagues, it is unlikely that he or she would ever be considered prime leadership material.

Intelligent legislators are creative and innovative; they foresee legislation or amendments that are needed and ably make their point before committees. They are able to answer the questions posed and plan the strategy necessary for a bill's passage. Personable legislators can persuade the committees, party caucuses, or party leaders of the need for particular legislation and, because of warm personal relations, their colleagues at times are willing to give them votes to help out.[26] Flexible legislators enjoy the "give and take" of the legislative arena and recognize the need for compromise. These people are careful to adhere to the norms of the legislature, and feel a great loyalty to it. Legislators having generous portions of these three attributes appear to be prime material for future leadership positions. Further, these differences became quickly apparent.

By the end of the first year, freshmen members of the class of '66 could identify within their own ranks colleagues whom they perceived as very effective. Freshmen were asked to suggest who among their colleagues in the freshman ranks had been most effective (we did not define this term, but let the legislator decide). There were many nominations, but some quite discernible patterns developed. Four freshmen were clearly perceived by their peers as being most influential, receiving ten to seventeen nominations from their colleagues. Twelve other freshmen could be defined as being on the fringes of effectiveness, having from two to seven nominations. Sixteen freshmen were perceived by their colleagues as being least effective; they had either no nominations or only one.[27] Of essential importance here is that there was some common (but unarticulated) frame of reference among the freshmen. Nominations were not random—there was substantial agreement about who was and who was not effective.

Period 4: Secondary Legislative Socialization

Exactly when the transformation from freshman to veteran occurs cannot be precisely stipulated.[28] The point of transition was different for each freshmen legislator; some quickly learned the ropes; others took much longer; and a few never seemed to acquire the status of veteran at all.[29]

Because of the advantages accruing to incumbents, most veteran legislators are able to get reelected without too much difficulty. It is true that some legislators retire, die, or get reapportioned out; others accept judicial positions, while still others move on to "higher" elective office—the state Senate, statewide office, or Congress. However, for those who want to remain in the state Assembly, getting reelected is not usually too difficult. Thus, most freshmen are reelected (and continue their legislative socialization).

ACCUMULATION

During this fourth period, legislators continue to learn their jobs. Most veteran legislators develop two prime areas of expertise: first, in some specific, complex subject-matter areas; and second, in the intricacies of the legislative process. The expertise in particular subject-matter areas derives from committee work in a specialized area on some topic such as water, education, criminal justice, the budget, or taxation. Normally, even with the periodic changes in Assembly leadership, veteran members get reassigned to committees on which they have developed an expertise. Consequently, expertise comes with years of committee work: listening to experts testify, discussions over committee bills, and carrying one's own bills before "your" committee.

The second area of expertise, the intricacies of the legislative process, depends upon acquiring a firm grasp of the formal and informal rules of the Assembly and the Senate, knowledge of the people who make key decisions in both houses, an awareness of the various alternatives in strategy that might be employed, and to some extent communication with the Governor's staff. In both areas of expertise, the veteran legislator has learned through experience and has a substantial advantage over the freshmen.

Legislators continued to develop some role orientations in period 4. In particular, the Assembly member's interest group and party roles exhibited considerable change. On the other hand, as we have seen, most of the representative role was well established by this time. During this phase, legislators continued to move toward the trustee, resister, and nonpartisan role orientations. While some of the changes were not substantial, they suggest that the process of role acquisition was not complete.

As discussed earlier, perceptions about the importance of legislative inputs were largely a product of pre-legislative life experience (about seventy percent), with the Speaker, committees, and committee chairmen continuing to rank as very important. A few factors considered not too crucial in the first and second interviews came to be considered more important by the third interview—i.e., the influence of state political parties and interest groups. On the other hand, a few factors dropped in perceived influence during period 4. Among those was the conflict between north and south. Several different factors continued to vie for the least important distinction; generally those ranking lowest were the local factors.

Legislative experience during the second year produced some consensus, overcoming the dissonance of the first year. But neither the patterns of consensus nor dissonance associated meaningfully with the veterans' perceptions. Perhaps the most significant finding about legislative experience is that it substantially altered consensual levels in such a way that no clear-cut pattern of change emerged. There was little relationship between initial levels of agreement and the levels two years later.

Prior to legislative service, party and ideology were not polarizing factors contributing to dissonance, but region was. After the second year, party associated strongly with assessments about county government and particularly with the Governor and the state Senate, but no longer with the important input factors of the first year; and ideology now associated meaningfully with the urban versus rural conflict, committees, and city government. But just as important, legislative experience reduced polarization or eliminated it in a number of cases. Most significantly, the generally supposed polarizing factors were not very meaningful. They exercised influence in only a few cases.

INTERPERSONAL TRANSFER

As legislators serve through the years, their talents become recognized by their colleagues. In time, some are selected to key positions on committees such as Ways and Means or Rules, as party leaders or as committee chairmen. While no elaborate inventory will be suggested here, it does seem apparent that the political, social, leadership, and occupational skills which were developed prior to legislative service could be transferred to the legislative arena and applied as party leader, member of a prestige committee, or committee chairmen. During their second session, and in particular, during their second term, freshmen had increasingly greater opportunities to demonstrate these skills. (Again, as in period 3, the reader is reminded that the concept of transfer has limited applicability.)

COGNITIVE-DEVELOPMENTAL

In the California Assembly, a legislator is not promoted or given advancements simply because (s)he has served many years and is a senior member. Rather, one must possess ability and energy, work hard, and get along well with fellow legislators (as discussed above). Thus, advancement in the Assembly power hierarchy is a good indicator of who possesses such qualities. (This does not mean that some who do not advance up the power hierarchy lack such qualities, but most likely they belong to the minority party! However, even minority party members can get elected to party positions, have a few committee chairmanships, and can get selected to some of the major committees or elected to the Rules Committee by their caucus.) We have defined the positions of major consequence in a descending order of importance. They are:

(1) Election to party leadership post—Speaker, Speaker ProTempore, majority or minority floor leader, or caucus leader.

(2) Selection as committee chairperson.

(3) Selection to the Ways and Means Committee or election to the Rules Committee.[30]

(4) Selection as subcommittee chairperson.

(5) Selection as vice chairperson.

We concede that some might contend that the positions of committee vice chairperson chairing a subcommittee are not really leadership posts of much consequence. Our view was that selection to one of these minor posts gave at least some indication that the individual was accepted by colleagues and the top leadership of the chambers.

Many of the members of the class of '66 moved into these key posts rather quickly. Others failed to be selected or elected to these positions. Why did this difference exist? Certainly, as noted in Chapter 4, considerable knowledge of the unwritten rules prior to legislative service did not guarantee rapid advancement. In fact, we found almost no correlation between initial knowledge of the rules of the game and subsequent legislative advancement. On the other hand, party control played a major role in affording opportunities for advancement. In 1968, the Republicans, after a long drought, captured control of the Assembly. There was an opportunity for the new Republican Speaker, Robert Monagan, to remove some of the Democratic committee chairmen and replace them with Republicans as well as giving Republicans working majorities on some of the key legislative committees.[31] Consequently, the dynamics of leadership promotion to these various positions can be analyzed more clearly on the Republican side. (A subsequent change in party control in 1970 fell outside the time frame of this analysis.)

The cognitive-developmental model helps give some of the reasons why particular legislators were appointed or not appointed to choice positions. Some legislators were not selected because they simply did not want the responsibility or pressures that these positions entailed, though they did have the ability. Others either did not have the political "savvy" or expertise in a particular subject matter area or did not have the needed support of their colleagues. Obviously, intelligence and personality were factors here.

It was our overall impression, however, that perhaps the most important factor was flexibility. Among those least likely to attain leadership positions were members clearly identified with either the militant liberal camp or the ultra-conservative group. Generally, members of these two informal factions seemed less concerned with the niceties of observing the rules of the game, and were more responsive to certain constituency or ideological pressures. They simply did not seem as concerned about "getting along" with their colleagues as did the others. Less concerned with expertise in particular subject matter areas and more likely to view their ideological opponents in pejorative terms, they were often unable to work with some of their colleagues. In short, they often had little respect or tolerance for others' positions.[32] Such legislators were not likely to be placed in positions of overall leadership.[33]

This is not to say that all new legislators should set their sights on becoming political effectives, joining the "club," or striving for a leadership position. Over a decade ago Ralph Huitt argued persuasively that the "outsider" in the U.S. Senate could play an important role in that chamber even without being a member of the governing establishment.[34] The ideologue and the more issue-oriented legislators have a meaningful role to play in the legislative process. They frequently initiate and carry some of the most controversial legislation of the session, and thus serve to help "kick off" discussion on highly sensitive issues. In short, those who are perceived as less effective, whether through lack of time, expertise, political "savvy," personality, flexibility or choice still have an important role to play in the legislature. Moreover, there would simply not be enough leadership positions in the Assembly to accommodate everyone if all had the inclination and ability to be leaders. The three alternative routes of period 4 help reduce potential conflict for these choice positions.

Leadership in the Assembly must learn to live with and accept the less effective legislators. While the bills that they carry can be held up or killed in committee, leadership must keep in mind the importance of their vote in committee, and on the floor. While they may not be selected as Speaker or minority party leader, they do have a vote in caucus. Moreover, legislators perceived as less effective by their colleagues may very well be quite popular in their home districts and may have little trouble getting reelected. Once every ten years, with the new census, it would be possible to punish these legislators by redrawing district lines, but this seems an extremely tenuous whip for the leadership to potentially wield. (Particularly since the courts have recently reapportioned state legislatures in California and elsewhere.) In sum, the "effectives," "backbenchers," and "mavericks" all have a role to play in the Assembly. The legislature is able to do its work because of the diverse goal balance of its membership.

Summary

Several years ago, Jack Dennis, in an extremely able and provocative article, contended that there were ten major problem areas in political socialization research. Dennis briefly summarized the problem dimensions as:

(1) system relevance of political socialization

(2) varieties of content of political socialization

(3) political socialization across the life cycle

(4) political socialization across generations

(5) cross-cultural aspects of political socialization

(6) subgroup and subcultural variations

(7) the political learning process

(8) the agents and agencies of political socialization

(9) the extent and relative effects of political socialization upon different individuals

(10) specialized—especially elite—political socialization.[35]

Though the present study touches upon almost all the areas listed above, the main thrust of the work centers on "specialized—especially elite—political socialization." Dennis contends, and we would heartily concur, that this is one of the least developed areas of political socialization research.

Dennis goes on to argue that, unlike other topics of political behavior research where data have far outstripped theory, socialization efforts thus far, for the most part, have attempted to link theory and data and have avoided what he terms "hyperfactualism."[36] Though this may reasonably describe political socialization research generally, it does not apply to elite socialization research where there is both a paucity of data and theoretical formulation to test, borrow, or adapt. We were able to use the Hess and Torney models of childhood political socialization in our study of elite socialization, though at times with obvious difficulty. In addition, we combined the Hess and Torney process models with our own period-phase model in trying to come to grips with the dimension of time. The greatest conceptual weakness was found in the application of the Hess and Torney transfer model. While very useful during the first two periods, it became potentially misleading in the third and fourth periods. This was certainly no fault of Professors Hess and Torney. Their model was developed to better understand childhood political socialization. It appears to us that transfer is a very important concept in such cases. But, in studying specific adult political socialization, the transfer model loses much of its utility because our methodology is inadequate. Further, the identification model is not particularly useful due to the limits of our data. On the whole, however, we feel that the theoretical framework we adopted and developed does make sense. Hopefully, further theoretical formulations on elite socialization will be able to keep pace with the rapidly accumulating data.

Certainly, one unique element in this study is the timing of our interviews. Most other studies of legislative recruitment and socialization have focused on the trials and tribulations of the new legislator after (s)he has joined the establishment. Previously, the pre-legislative aspects of legislative socialization (which were recognized as important by various authorities) had to be derived by implication or from the recollections of legislators. Obviously, attempting to recall various facets of one's pre-legislative career is not nearly as useful as interviewing the person before (s)he is a legislator. In this study, we are able to push legislative socialization analysis back a stage, to the transitional period. It is our belief that this adds significantly to our understanding of the process of elite socialization and the legislative process. We are able to measure changes that took place in role development, rule knowledge, and input perceptions. We were also able to determine the direction of the changes and, in a corollary vein, assess the impact of several selected, supposedly socializing agents. Among these agents were party, region, ideology, formal and informal groups, and veterans.

It seems apparent that if we are to understand how legislatures operate, we must understand the process of legislative socialization —the adaptation to legislative service. We have considered this process to be a continuous one, which begins with the basic democratic political socialization experienced by most citizens in early childhood, followed by the growing political activism and candidacy experienced by only a few citizens, and finally the relatively unique experience of election, the first year of legislative experience, and lastly, entry into the status of seasoned veteran. In this process, the initial political socializing agencies of family, school, church, and peer group are complemented before election by community, party, and campaign experiences and after election by the legislative socialization agencies of individuals and groups which are part of the legislative milieu. It is from *all these sources* that the formal and informal rules, roles, perceptions, and the norms of the institution are passed on to the newcomer.

By understanding the process of legislative socialization, one is better able to appreciate the considerable resistance to change or reform which is found in our state legislatures (as well as Congress and other collegial political institutions). In their legislative process text, William J. Keefe and Morris S. Ogul discuss the various criticisms that are directed toward American legislatures. They assert that no other criticism is made more frequently and persistently than: "The legislature is not sufficiently responsive to majority preferences either in the electorate or *within the institution itself.*"[37] Clearly, this latter charge did not appear to be totally the case in California in 1967. In the Assembly, with almost one-half of the membership freshmen, the leadership made every attempt to placate and accommodate itself to the new power factor. In a sense, the large bloc of new legislators also socialized the veteran legislators. (In the upper house, the Senate leadership failed to accommodate themselves to new members and subsequently lost their positions in the legislature).

The point is that, while socialization is inherently a pattern-maintaining process of newcomers learning from veterans, it is not a rigid one-way street. Legislatures do change (though some cynics would contend, imperceptibly), new leadership emerges, some rules of the game are discarded, some are added, and veterans must learn to live with and accommodate themselves to the freshmen and vice versa. In short, the legislative socialization process is not static; legislative leaders must learn to bend with the times and make adjustments to internal critics and new external forces. This is particularly true in legislative bodies not adhering to the seniority principle, such as California's Assembly and, perhaps to a growing extent, the U.S. Congress.

Lastly, we have found that what the new legislator brings with him from previous life experiences is critically important in both his role as representative and in his perceptions of the legislature. If there is a rigidity in our state legislatures, it can probably be accounted for more by the recruitment process than by internal socialization processes.[38]

NOTES

1. See our discussion of this in Chapter 2, pp. 29-35 and in Chapter 3.

2. Robert D. Hess and Judith V. Torney, *The Development of Political Attitudes in Children* (Garden City, N.Y.: Doubleday Anchor, 1968), p. 22.

3. The description of the four models paraphrases the discussion in Hess and Torney, ibid., pp. 22-26.

4. In the State Legislative Research Project, the authors report that these primary groups may have slightly *less* impact in California—perhaps, it is speculated, because primary group influence is predicated on substantial population stability and in California there is considerable mobility. The differences among the four states of the Research Project on the percentage of legislators citing primary groups as socializing agencies were as follows: California, thirty-four percent; New Jersey, forty-seven percent; Ohio, forty-three percent; and Tennessee, forty-two percent. See John C. Wahlke, Heinz Eulau, William Buchanan, and LeRoy C. Ferguson, *The Legislative System* (New York: John Wiley, 1962), pp. 79-80.

5. In the State Legislative Research Project, it was reported that forty percent of California legislators had recalled their earliest political interest from the childhood or grammar school period. Our smaller number, six or nineteen percent, appears to be markedly lower. However, we asked when the respondent had first become active in politics. Wahlke, et al. asked when the respondent had become interested in politics; see *The Legislative System,* p. 81.

6. Hess and Torney, *The Development of Political Attitudes in Children,* pp. 222, 195.

7. Ibid., p. 171.

8. Kenneth P. Langton and M. Kent Jennings, "Political Socialization and the High School Civics Curriculum in the United States," *American Political Science Review* LXII, No. 3 (September, 1968), p. 866.

9. Certainly some of this country's most prominent presidents, U.S. senators, and governors have been elected to their positions with negligible political experience.

10. Lester W. Milbrath, *Politics in the American States,* Herbert Jacob and Kenneth Vines, eds. (Boston: Little, Brown, 1965), p. 28.

11. James David Barber, *The Lawmakers* (New Haven: Yale University Press, 1965) p. 223.

12. For an extremely interesting discussion of the role of the lawyer in the legislature and the skills brought to the legislative arena, see Leonard I. Ruchelman, "Lawyers in the New York State Legislature," *Midwest Journal of Political Science,* Vol. 10 (November 1966), pp. 484-497. Beverly Blair Cook reports that California judges quite often have backgrounds of political activity, with thirty-two percent of judges having

Figure 7.2: A Phase-Process Model of Legislative Socialization

Process:	Preparatory Legislative Socialization Phase		Specific Legislative Socialization Phase	
	Basic Socialization Period	Transitional Socialization Period	Initial Legislative Socialization Period	Secondary Legislative Socialization Period
Accumulation	Basic knowledge and values acquired. Rep. role orientation develops	Acquires more political knowledge. Learns about campaigns. Acquires a substantial proportion of input perceptions. Some input perceptions polarized by region. Develops some initial unstable party and interest group roles	Some modification of Rep. role. Interest group role begins to develop, about 1/3rd. Party role begins to develop, about 1/2. Some input perceptions modified (governor and federal government). Greater disagreement about inputs—party and region account for some polarization. Begins to acquire some process expertise. Acquires additional policy information	Acquires substantial policy knowledge. Party role stabilizes. Interest group role continues to develop and starts to stabilize. A few changes in input perceptions. Some input consensus develops. Party and ideology polarize some input perceptions, region no longer meaningful
Interpersonal	Learns the general "newcomer" role. Acquires some general fundamentals of the rules of the game	Some begin to acquire knowledge about political interpersonal rules of the game (usually liberals and democrats)	Knowledge about interpersonal rules of the game brought up to par. Substantial learning about legislative rules of the game	Acquires additional sophistication in rules of the game. Acquires additional process knowledge
Identification	Some imitation of admired individuals	More intense exposure to political personalities	Some veterans provide legislative models	Unknown
Cognitive-Developmental	Not applicable	Not applicable	The limits of ability, energy and personality begin to be observed	Limits become quite visible, particularly in "effectiveness". Slow advancement or no advancement into positions of legislative leadership

held elective public office. See her book, *The Judicial Process in California* (Belmont, Calif.: Dickenson, 1967), p. 45.

13. The literature in this area is fairly extensive. Perhaps the classic study of politics and the professional public relations firm is Stanley Kelley, Jr., *Professional Public Relations and Political Power* (Baltimore: Johns Hopkins Press, 1956).

14. We are struck by the fact that several contemporary politicians appear to have picked the John F. Kennedy look, gestures, and speaking style.

15. Technically, the new legislator filed a campaign statement within thirty-five days of election with the Secretary of state and the County Clerk of the county in which (s)he resides. The Secretary of State then issued a certificate of election which was prima facie evidence of his or her right to membership. See James D. Driscoll, *California's Legislature* (Sacramento: State Printing Office), p. 68.

16. As was mentioned previously, in most ways, the legislator elect began to take on the duties and enjoy the prerequisites of being a lawmaker months before they were actually sworn in.

17. Surprisingly, a rather large proportion of the class were either unmarried, divorced, or were at that point in their lives when the children had left home, and they did not have to face this decision.

18. One freshman legislator in 1971 attempted to work out a compromise on the matter. He flew from Los Angeles to Sacramento and back every day! Even for Californians, this is a rather lengthy commute.

19. See "Times Have Changes: Half of Legislators Now Make Sacramento Home," *California Journal,* IV, No. 4 (April 1973), pp. 121-122.

20. On this point in our first interview, conducted before the freshmen had taken office, we asked how many hours per week they thought they would spend on the job while the legislature was in session. As we anticipated, the candidates-elect underestimated the amount of time they would be working on legislative matters. In the second interview, after a year's service on the average, respondents estimated they spent about sixty-one hours per week on the job. Before service, they had estimated an average of fifty-six hours.

21. Perhaps we should include here several freshman legislators themselves, especially those who were former legislative staff employees. These members at times perceived their roles in the first term as a sort of bridge between the sizable freshman class and the veteran members. (This role also gave them more influence than they otherwise would have had.)

22. The contrast in style between the California Assembly and the U.S. House of Representatives is considerable. In 1970, Allard K. Lowenstein, a leader in the New Politics movement nationally and the former National Chairman for the Eugene McCarthy presidential campaign (but also a House freshman) attempted to get recognized on the House floor when they were debating a congressional resolution dealing with President Richard Nixon's Cambodian action. After attempting repeatedly all afternoon to gain recognition from the presiding officer, Rep. Lowenstein was in the very late afternoon allowed to speak. He was given forty-five seconds to discuss this topic. See Sacramento *Bee,* May 13, 1970.

Interestingly, some of the bitterest and most vociferous recent critics of the seniority system in Congress have been several California Congressmen who formerly had served in the California legislature; for example, Representatives Jerome Waldie, Tom Rees, and Eugene Burkhalter.

23. Members of the class of '66 were in overwhelming agreement that they had been accorded better treatment as newcomers because of the size of their class and because of

the particularly high caliber of their members. They felt that the new freshmen (the class of '68) would be accorded approximately similar treatment, though not quite as generous. Interestingly, in a somewhat chauvinistic but perhaps accurate assessment of the class of '68, several members of the class of '66 asserted that the members of their own class had been better prepared. Certainly, the class of '68 did not have the opportunities of the class of '66.

24. A new group formed in the legislature in 1970, the Environmental Caucus, undoubtedly should be included with the other groups.

25. The size of the class, the number of committees, the paucity of "veterans-only" committees (i.e., Ways and Means and Rules), and the insignificance of seniority all contributed to the ease with which the Speaker could make committee selections. Though there are always grumbles about particular people not getting what they think they should, generally committee assignments have not been *too* bothersome an issue in the state Assembly. However, Republicans in 1971 seemed particularly bitter about their lot. One Republican legislator even charged Speaker Moretti with using Mafia-like tactics in his assignments.

26. While hard to quantify, we are convinced that, except on ideological or party issues, legislators will give one of their colleagues a vote just because they like him or her, and deny it to one they do not like.

27. It should be noted that our n here is 32. This is because freshmen not participating in our first and second interviews could nevertheless be included in the effectiveness ratings by their colleagues.

28. It is interesting to note that in California the major positions of responsibility are not held by the most senior Assembly members. Generally, sophomores and juniors are the major work horses in the Assembly.

29. Some of the newcomers perceived themselves as veterans after only a few months of service in the legislature; others thought of themselves as veterans after the first session (the first year), and still others continued to view themselves in a sort of freshman status well into their second term. To explore this topic, we asked the successfully reelected members of the class of '66 (only two failed to survive) in our third interview whether they now considered themselves "veterans." Most of the class felt that they were now veterans; they had been "blooded," as one member put it. Approximately one-third viewed themselves in transitional terms such as—"I'm a sophomore." Two said that they thought of themselves as veterans, but one felt some of the senior Senators (members of the other house) did not share this attitude; another felt some of the senior Assemblymen did not share this sentiment. The members of the class of '66 did not couch their replies to this question in decidedly inferior status terms, such as suggesting that they still had to prove themselves, or that they still had a long way to go. In short, the apprenticeship period seems much shorter for California legislators than it does for Congressmen.

.30. The Assembly Rules Committee is the only committee not selected by the Speaker. Members are chosen by the two party caucuses, although the Speaker does select the chairperson of this committee.

31. In all, Speaker Monagan selected fifteen Republican and six Democratic committee chairpersons. Republicans outnumbered Democrats on Ways and Means by an eleven to eight margin and Rules by a four to three margin.

32. It is true that, in the 1971 legislative session some of the militant liberals were given choice committee assignments. None of these was from the class of '66.

33. Stephen V. Monsma argued similarly, "The structure of interpersonal relations within legislative systems functions to place legislators with high degrees of skill and

conscientiousness in the center of the legislative system and to increase their influence, and to isolate legislators with low degrees of skill and conscientiousness on the periphery of the legislative system and to decrease their influence." See "Interpersonal Relations in the Legislative System: A Study of the 1964 Michigan House of Representatives," *Midwest Journal of Political Science,* X, No. 3 (August 1966), pp. 350-363.

34. Ralph Huitt, "The Outsider in the United States Senate," *American Political Science Review,* LV, No. 3 (September 1961), pp. 566-575.

35. Jack Dennis, "Major Problems of Political Socialization Research," *Midwest Journal of Political Science,* XII, No. 1 (February 1968), p. 110.

36. Ibid., p. 87.

37. William J. Keefe and Morris S. Ogul, *The American Legislative Process: Congress and the States* (Englewood Cliffs, N.J.: Prentice-Hall, 1968), p. 5.

38. Two recent studies of the impact of "professionalism" and "effectiveness" on state's legislatures suggest that neither has had a very substantial effect. See Joel M. Fisher, Charles M. Price, and Charles G. Bell, *The Legislative Process in California* (Washington, D.C.: American Political Science Association, 1973) and Leonard G. Ritt, "State Legislative Reform: Does It Matter?" *American Politics Quarterly,* Vol. 1, No. 4 (October 1973), pp. 499-510.

APPENDIX A:

Research Methodology

The research reported herein took advantage of an unusual situation which occurred in California in 1965. During that year, the state legislature was required to reapportion both houses on the basis of population in conformity to a series of court decisions which had begun with Baker v. Carr in 1962. As a result, California's upper house, which had been previously apportioned on the basis of county lines, was reapportioned on an equal-population basis. The political impact was staggering. Los Angeles County alone acquired thirteen new state senators (thirty-two percent of the total chamber) with the other populous counties (Orange, San Diego, San Francisco, Alameda, and Santa Clara) also receiving substantial increments in representation. On the other hand, well over half of California's counties lost some or most of their previous representation in the state Senate.[1] The Assembly, which had been apportioned on the basis of population, felt the impact of reapportionment only indirectly, when a number of Assemblymen decided in late 1965 and early 1966 to seek election to the more prestigious Senate. Twenty-one Assembly seats were vacated in this massive game of political musical chairs. In addition, one Assemblyman ran for statewide office, six retired, and one died in office. Thus, in all, there were twenty-nine open districts from which *a freshman had to be elected.*

The Research Design

PANEL DESIGN

Since the major focus of our study was the process of legislative socialization, we decided to employ a "before and after" survey design. Eventually, this meant interviewing the same respondents three times—first, before they had had any experience as legislators and twice after they had served in the California Assembly (see Figure A.1). The assumptions of such a design are that: (1) data gathered during the first interviews are the result of pre-legislative experience, (2) that data gathered during the subsequent interviews are partially the result of the intervening variable of legislative experience, and that (3) it is possible to sort out the impact of such legislative experience. The first set of interviews was gathered during September-December 1966—most of them prior to the November elections (see Table A.1). These interviews gave us the essential "before" data. A second set of interviews was gathered following the freshman's first year of legislative experience. The third set of interviews was gathered after the freshmen had been reelected in

"BEFORE"	"INTERVENING VARIABLE"	"AFTER" A	"INTERVENING VARIABLE"	"AFTER" B	"BENCH MARK"
Interview I		Interview II		Interview III	Interview V
Potential Freshman Interviewed	Freshman serves a year in the California Assembly	Freshmen Interviewed Again	Freshman serves a second year in the California Assembly	Freshmen Interviewed for a third time	Veterans Interviewed
Pre-service data gathered		Legislative experience data gathered		Same Questions asked for a second time	Same questions asked of the Veterans
Measures pre-service attitudes, values, role orientations and perceptions		Measures the same variables as in first interview		Measures the same variables as in first and second interviews	Measures the same variables as in freshman interviews

Figure A.1: THE PANEL DESIGN

Table A.1: Schedule and Length of Interviews

Panel	Number of Respondents	Type	Period of Time	Length of Interviews Minimum	Maximum	Average
I	26	Winners	Sept.-Oct. 1966	50 min.	110 min.	63 min.
	6 (32****)	Winners*	December 1966	60 min.	80 min.	78 min.
	16	Losers	Sept.-Oct. 1966	50 min.	120 min.	69 min.
II	33	One-Year Freshmen	Dec. '67-Feb. '68	40 min.	125 min.	79 min.
III	31	One-Term Freshmen	Jan.-March 1969	15 min.	60 min.	30 min.
V**	34	Veterans***	Feb.-March 1969 and Sept. 1969	18 min.	90 min.	36 min.

(48 = 26, 6, 16)

*These were the unexpected winners.
**We have used the "V" for veterans rather than the IV for the fourth panel.
***Veterans were those who had been elected any time prior to November 1966.
****As discussed elsewhere, one of these was dropped from the tabulation.

1968. (Two of the freshman members of the class of '66 were defeated in the elections of 1968; a fourth set of interviews, using comparable questions, was gathered from thirty-four [71%] of the veterans. These data gave us additional information facilitating the analysis of legislative socialization.)

PANEL PROBLEMS

While the "before and after" design is a substantial improvement over the more usual "after only" design, there are two problems associated with this type of study which the reader should recognize.[2] First, the use of the "before" or pre-test interview may well contaminate subsequent interviews. Our respondents had been informed that they would be interviewed again approximately a year after the first interview. While we were careful not to specifically state or imply that any of the questions used in the first interview would be used in the later interviews, it is certainly possible that some of the legislators may have been sensitized to the issues raised by the items. While there was no way for the legislators to "study" for the next interview, the possibility of contamination must be recognized.[3]

The second problem associated with our particular use of the "before and after" design is that there was no "pure" control group. There were, in a sense, however, two quasi-control groups available—the losers and the veterans. Use of the losers as a control group would have allowed us to assess contamination. However, use of this group would have required a second round of interviews throughout the state, which was beyond our means. The second quasi-control group, the veterans, we did use.

MEASURING CHANGE

The ability to measure change was crucial to our study. In order to assess the impact of legislative experience upon legislative roles and perceptions we had to not only identify and measure such variables before and after legislative service, but we had to be able to express such changes in quantitative terms. (The specific techniques used, chi-square, standard deviation, or various measures of association are discussed as they are applied during the body of this book.) The "before and after" measures are, we feel, a substantial improvement on other legislative behavior research which has uniformly employed a single set of interviews with incumbent lawmakers. Thus, with no measures of roles, attitudes, or perceptions prior to legislative service, the findings of Wahlke et al., Kornberg, Sorauf, Eulau, Patterson, and others have been limited to analyses and descriptions at a particular point in time during legislative service. Of course, this has not prevented these researchers from making insightful and useful suggestions about the nature and dynamics of legislative experience. Indeed, it is from these earlier efforts that many of our own hypotheses have been drawn.

IDENTIFYING POTENTIAL FRESHMEN

Our panel of potential freshmen was largely drawn from the open districts discussed above. However, the panel was enlarged somewhat by including challengers in certain districts where circumstances appeared to threaten the incumbent. Specific identification of potential freshmen to be interviewed occurred after the June 1966 primary elections. While we would have preferred to have interviewed potential freshmen prior to the primary elections, it was not physically possible. Three hundred forty-three potential freshmen (nonincumbents) ran in the 1966 primary elections. This large number was due in great measure to the many "open" districts that year. Only 114 challengers ran in the fifty-one districts with incumbents (an average of 3.2 candidates). But, 229 ran in the twenty-nine districts with no incumbents (an average of 7.0 candidates per district). With such a large number, we were forced to wait until after the primary elections to begin interviewing potential freshmen.

The field was substantially reduced after the primary—to fifty-seven candidates running in the twenty-nine open districts (one district was so one-sided that the minority party had no candidate). In nineteen districts (out of the twenty-nine) one of the two major candidates appeared to be in such a strong position that we did not interview the other candidate. This further reduced our panel of potential freshmen to thirty-eight. We also added four candidates in districts where we thought the incumbent might be in danger of defeat. (The reader may wonder why we tried so hard to reduce the number of interviews. Simply put, the two of us had about six weeks to gather the data, and California is a very large state.) This enlarged our pre-election panel of potential freshmen Assembly members to a total of forty-two. However, as might be expected, our pre-election assessments were not 100% correct.[4] Five incumbents were unexpectedly defeated, and we were in error in making "one-party" assessments in two districts. Fortunately, six of the seven unexpected winners granted interviews shortly after the November elections. Thus, since we had had only one refusal from the preelection panel, we were able to secure a total of forty-seven interviews. Of these, thirty-one were sworn in as freshmen Assembly members in January 1967. (One of our respondents had served in the California Assembly several years earlier—though interviewed, we have eliminated his responses from our analysis in this book. Including him would have increased the number to thirty-two. The two candidates who refused interviews were also elected. Our final sample constitutes ninety-four percent of the universe of freshmen.)

CONTENT OF INTERVIEWS

The major thrust of this study has been presented earlier, and the specific interview questions are presented in the following appendices. However, a brief overview is in order here. A substantial proportion of each interview was devoted to the respondents' role orientations, perceptions, and knowledge of the rules of the game. Repetition of standardized questions dealing with these areas was essential to our study of the socialization process—thus, each questionnaire contained these same items (see the other appendices for the copies of the questionnaires). In addition, in each interview we gathered other appropriate data. During the first interview (before service in the Assembly), we gathered a substantial amount of standard demographic data; age, race, sex, socioeconomic information; political, community, and religious activity; and employment history, for example. Naturally, these questions were not repeated during the later set of interviews.

During the second set of interviews, we replaced the demographic questions with items about the freshman's first-year difficulties, whom he or she sought help from, initial relationships with the press and lobbies, and how each respondent was handling constituency problems. The third set of interviews was much shorter—they were essentially only the standardized items. A careful reading of the questionnaires will reveal that many questions have been used by other researchers (e.g., the role items developed by Wahlke et al.). While we had to make minor word changes in some cases, we feel that we were able to collect our data in such a form that it is essentially comparable to earlier findings.

LOCATION OF FIRST INTERVIEWS

Initial interviews were always by appointment—usually at the candidate's place of work (45%) or at campaign headquarters (30%). A few interviews were held in the candidates' homes (15%) while the remainder were gathered in such diverse places as bars, restaurants, garden parties, or while traveling in a car. It is interesting to note that those respondents who lost met us at their headquarters less frequently (19%) than those who subsequently won (40%). Concomitantly, losers were more likely to have been interviewed in their homes (31%) compared to winners (4%). We suspect that these differences may reflect different levels of campaign activity between winners and losers.

LOCATION OF SUBSEQUENT INTERVIEWS

California's Assembly members are provided office suites in the state's capitol. Since the legislature meets most of the year, we quickly found that it was more efficient to interview incumbents in Sacramento than to travel about the state seeking legislators at home. Thus, our second and third interviews with the class of '66 (and with veterans) were almost all secured at the capitol.

Typically, we would arrive early in the week, make interview appointments through the Assembly members' secretaries and hope that they could keep the appointments. Since legislators are very busy, we found it best to have one of us available at all times during the day—we seldom scheduled two interviews at the same time. We also found it best to schedule interviews two hours apart. This gave us the flexibility needed if the legislator arrived late for the interview or if the interview ran over time. Finally, we found that the early session weeks—late January to early March—were the best time to secure interviews. By late March, the pace of legislative affairs was too brisk to permit hour-long interviews.

RAPPORT WITH RESPONDENTS

We were able to achieve good rapport with the class of '66 in several ways. First, we wrote to each potential freshman in the summer of 1966 explaining the project and informing them that we would soon phone for an appointment. Second, each candidate was given the usual assurances of anonymity. Third, we asked no questions about campaign issues. Fourth, we were careful not to overstay our welcomes—we promised each respondent that the interview would take one hour. While a few lasted longer, it was clear that such sessions were enjoyable to the respondent. Fifth, all interviews were conducted by one of the authors—no research assistant or graduate assistant was used. At this stage of the study, our respondents had not yet achieved the status of legislator and were flattered and impressed that a college professor wanted their opinions and views. Sixth, respondents were told that they would be reinterviewed at a later data (winners only). Thus, it was early established that the 1966 interviews were a part of a long-term project. And, seventh, the questions we asked about representational roles, perceptions of the importance of the Governor in the legislative process, the rules of the game, etc., were interesting to the respondents. We were asking them questions about a subject they were very much concerned with—the legislative process. As a result, not only did we get initial interviews from all but two members of the class of '66, but subsequently we were able to reinterview everyone initially interviewed—this was crucial to our study.

NOTES

1. For an extensive discussion of the impact of reapportionment and reactions to it, see "Reapportionment in California: Consultants' Report to the Assembly," Assembly Committee on Elections and Reapportionment Report, Vol. 7, No. 9 (April 1965). Also

see Totten J. Anderson and Eugene C. Lee, "The 1966 Election in California," *Western Political Quarterly,* XX (June 1967), part 2, pp. 535-554.

2. For a summary of the problems associated with the "before and after" design, see R. L. Soloman, "An Extension of Control Group Design," *Psychological Bulletin,* XLVI (March 1949), pp. 137-150; Marie Jahoda et al., *Research Methods in Social Relations* (New York: Dryden Press, 1951), pp. 63-74; and Chester A. Insko, *Theories of Attitude Change* (New York: Appleton-Century-Crofts, 1967), pp. 3-6.

3. D. Campbell has suggested the use of what he calls a "post-test only" control group design, which uses two randomly selected groups, one of which is subjected to the variable being examined while the other is not. Both receive a post-test but no pre-test. This design has every advantage of the pre-test/post-test design and avoids the problem of pre-test contamination. See D. Campbell, "Factors Relative to the Validity of Experiments in Social Settings," *Psychology Bulletin,* Vol. 54 (July 1957), pp. 297-312.

4. For a full description of the 1966 elections see Anderson and Lee, op. cit.

APPENDIX B:

Legislative Socialization Survey
Schedule Number One

((By observation record Respondent's))

                          SEX: M_____ F_____
                          RACE: _____

First, we'd like some general background data:

(1) Year of birth_____

(2) Place of Birth: City_____ County_____

     State_____ Nation (if not U.S.)_____

(3) Where were you brought up? City_____

     County_____ State_____

     Nation (if not U.S.)_____

(4) How long have you lived at your present address?

     _____years.

     How long have you lived in this area? _____years.

(if appropriate) Where did you live before moving here?

     City_____ State_____

(5) What is your principal occupation? (probe)

(if needed) What kind of work is that?

(6) Has this been your occupation all your working life?

     Yes_____ No_____

(if no) What other work have you done?

(The occupation answers should give you a good lead into this
series of questions)

(7) Where did you go to high school? City_____

     State_____

(if needed) Did you graduate? Yes_____ No_____

     Where did you go to college? City_____

     State_____

Name of College_____

What was your major in college?_____

Did you graduate? Yes_____ No_____

(Again, occupation will tell you if the post-grad questions are needed)

(if R is an attorney) Where did you go to law school?

City_____ State_____

Name of school_____

Have you done any post-graduate work? Yes_____ No_____

(if yes) Where?_____.

Name of school_____

Did you get any advanced degrees?

(8) What was your father's major occupation?

(if needed) What kind of work is that?

(9) Compared to your father, do you feel you are doing as well in life? Yes_____ No_____ Better_____ About the same_____ Worse_____

(10) Generally speaking, have you done as well in life up to now as you had hoped? Yes_____ No_____ Better_____ About the same_____ Worse_____

(show R auxilliary form I)

Now, I'd like to show you an attitude measuring device called a self-anchoring scale. You can see that we have not described the alternatives with words but with numbers, or scale values, zero through ten. Zero is the bottom and ten the top.

(11) As of now, where would you put yourself on this achievement ladder?_____

(12)   What is the highest point on this ladder that you could
       reasonably hope to achieve?_____

(show R auxilliary form II)

(13)   Using this modified self-anchoring scale, where would
       you put yourself on the social class scale?_____

A few minutes ago I asked how long you have lived in this community. Now I'd like to ask a few questions about your community activities.

(14)   About how many community or voluntary associations, like
       the Community Chest, Kiwanis or Masons, do you belong
       to now?_____

(15)   About how many meetings of these groups did you attend
       in the last four weeks?_____

(16)   Are you an officer in any of these groups? Yes_____
       No_____ (if yes) What positions do you hold?

               Group Name   Position

       _____   _____

       _____   _____

       _____   _____

       _____   _____

(17)   Are you a member of any religious denomination? Yes_____
       No_____

(if no, skip to #18)

       In the last month, how many times have you been able to
       attend religious services?_____

(if R has not mentioned his religious affiliation)

       May I ask what is your religious affiliation?_____

       (don't push this item)

We'd like to know some things about your previous political
activities, before you began your campaign for the Assembly.

(18)   When were you first active in politics? _____ year

(19)   Have you run for elective office before? Yes_____
       No_____   (if yes)

What	When	Where	Were you elected?
_____	_____	_____	_____
_____	_____	_____	_____
_____	_____	_____	_____
_____	_____	_____	_____

(20)   Have you been active in other campaigns? Yes_____
       No_____   (if yes, get the most recent four campaigns)

What	When	Where
_____	_____	_____
_____	_____	_____
_____	_____	_____
_____	_____	_____

(21)   How many campaigns, altogether, have you been active
       in?_____

(22)   Were you a member of a political club before you decided
       to run for the assembly? Yes_____   No_____

(23)   Were you active in that club? Yes_____   No_____
(this may cover part of answers you have received from #20)

(24)   Have you given money to other campaigns? Yes_____
       No_____

(25)   Have you held office in the Republican or Democratic

Party in the past? Yes_____   No_____

(if yes) What? (get four most recent)

What	When	Where
_____	_____	_____
_____	_____	_____
_____	_____	_____
_____	_____	_____

How many party offices have you held altogether?

(26) Have you held appointive office in the past? Yes_____

No_____

(if yes) What? (get four most recent)

What	When	Where
_____	_____	_____
_____	_____	_____
_____	_____	_____
_____	_____	_____

(27) When did you start to think about running for the
      Assembly? (Probe)

(28) If you are elected in November, do you think you will run
      for re-election in two years? Yes_____   No_____

(if no) Why not? (Probe)

(29) If you are elected in November do you think you might run
      for some other higher office? Yes_____   No_____

(if no or yes) Why? (Probe)

(30) If you are not elected this November, do you think you
      might run again? (Do not specify which office) Yes____

No_____

(if yes) What?

(31) What are some of the more enjoyable things about running
      for public office? (Probe)

(32) What are some of the things you like least about running
      for public office? (Probe)

(33) Using these self-anchoring scales again, how would you
      rate running for public office?

(Form III)_____

(Form IV)_____

(34) Looking at the job of being an Assemblyman, how many hours
      per week do you think you will spend on the job while
      the legislature is in session?_____

(35) Similarly, how many hours per week do you think you will
      spend on the job when the legislature is not in session?

      _____

(36) How much do you think it will cost you, in terms of lost
      income, to serve in the legislature?_____

Turning to the legislature, and what it does, we have been
told that the legislative process, what happens during the
session, is influenced by many things--for example, sectionalism, party, the governor, interest groups, etc. Using this
self-anchoring scale (Form V) how much influence do you think
the sectionalism of North v. South has?

(37)   _____

(38) Sectionalism--Urban v. Rural   _____

(39) Sectionalism--City v. Suburb   _____

(40) City Government   _____

(41) County Government   _____

(42) Local Businessmen   _____

(43) Local Labor Leaders   _____

(44) Local Community Leaders   _____

(45) Local Political Leaders   _____

(46) Political Parties   _____

(47) The Minority Party Leader   _____

(48) The Speaker in general, not

      the present incumbent   _____

(49) Committees   _____

(50) Committee Chairmen   _____

              If he is Reagan   _____

(51) The Governor   _____

              If he is Brown   _____

(52) The Bureaucracy   _____

(53) The State Senate   _____

(54) The Federal Government   _____

(55) Interest Groups   _____

(56) Parliamentary Procedure   _____

(57) Each Legislator's Own

      Ideology   _____

(58) How about your own political ideology, where would you

      put yourself on this scale?

(Form VI)   _____

(59) Going back to the Speaker, there have been rumors that

the present Speaker may have opposition in his bid for
re-election next January. What effect would it have on
your activities as an Assemblyman if you voted for the
losing candidate? (Probe)

(60) Going back to interest groups, to your knowledge, which
interest groups are most influential in California at
the present time?

(Get names)

(61) To your knowledge, which interest groups are most
influential in your own district at the present time?

(Get names)

(62) Looking at the Assembly, which committees do you think
are the most influential? (Get names)

We have been told that the Assembly, like most groups, has its
own unofficial rules, the Rules of the Game, things members
should do and should not do if they want the respect and
cooperation of other members.

(63) What are some of the Rules of the Game that you expect
to find in the Assembly? (Probe)

(64) How are these rules enforced? (Probe)

(65) Would you indicate on this scale how important are
these rules of the game? (Form V)_____

Now, looking at what you will be doing in Sacramento next
spring:

(66) When you go to Sacramento, will you take your wife with
you? Yes_____ No_____

(67) Will you take your children with you? Yes_____

      No_____

      Has no children_____ Children are "of age"_____

(68) When you get to Sacramento is there anyone you expect
      will help you learn the ropes, how to do your job?
      (Probe for names only)

(69) What committees would you like to be appointed to?
      (Don't probe)

(70) Is there a field of public policy that you are most
      interested in? (Probe)

(71) Is there a field of public policy that you feel you have
      a good deal of knowledge about? (Don't probe)

(72) How important do you think it is to be a specialist, an
      expert, in a particular area of legislation?(Form V)

      _____

(73) Specifically, why do you want to be a member of the
      Assembly? (Probe and then probe some more)

Now, I'd like to read you several statements. Will you please
indicate on this scale how strongly you agree or disagree with
each statement. (Form VII)

(74)A The job of an Assemblyman is to work for what his
      constituents want even though this may not always agree
      with his personal view. _____

    B The legislature is a full time job._____

    C Under our form of government, every individual should
      take an interest in government directly, not through

interest group organizations. _____

D The best interest of the people would be better served
  if Assemblymen were elected without party labels.

  _____

E The salaries of Assemblymen ought to be substantially
  increased. _____

F I expect interest groups or their agents will give me
  valuable help in lining-up support for my bills.

  _____

G An Assemblyman can decide how to vote on most issues by
  asking himself if the proposed law is morally right.

  _____

H If a bill is important for his party's record, an
  Assemblyman should vote with his party even if it costs
  him some support in his district. _____

I The legislature should meet most of the year, like
  Congress. _____

J I will seldom have to sound out my constituents because
  I think so much like them that I know how to react to
  almost any proposal. _____

K More staff and research facilities should be available
  to the Assembly. _____

L I expect to get valuable help in drafting bills or amendments from interest groups or their agents.

  _____

M It's just as important to be on guard against ideas put

out by people of one's own party as against ideas put
out by people in the opposite party. _____

N With his better sources of information, an Assemblyman
should vote as he thinks best even when his constituents
disagree.   _____

O Under our form of government, every individual should
take an interest in government directly, not through a
political party.   _____

P Interest groups have entirely too much influence in the
California Legislature today.   _____

(75) We have been told that legislative work is done in many
different places. How significant do you think the work
is that gets done in each of these places? (Form V)

    A. The floor of the Assembly   _____

    B. The halls of the Assembly   _____

    C. The committee sessions   _____

    D. The informal social gatherings   _____

    E. The party caucuses   _____

(76) This is the end of my regular questions. Is there anything that you would like to add?

Finish the Q on this page after the interview is over.

(77) Were other persons present within earshot during the interview? Yes_____ No_____

(78) Interviewer's estimate of respondent's frankness:
Very frank_____ Frank_____ Not very frank_____
Very evasive_____

(79) Interviewer's estimate of respondent's cooperation during the interview.
Very co-op._____ Co-op._____ Not very co-op._____
Very Un-co-op._____

(80) Any other comments by interviewer:

(81) Location of interview: Respondent's home_____
Respondent's place of work_____
Respondent's campaign headquarters_____
Other_____

(82) Time of interview--Time Began_____
Time Ended_____

(83) Date of interview_____

APPENDIX C:

Legislative Socialization Survey
Schedule Number Two

We have taken out the background questions from this second interview--aside from the first few questions it is the same as the one which we used last year.

(1) When you got to Sacramento last January, was there anyone who helped you learn the ropes, how to do your job? Who were they? (List-get names)

(2) What kinds of things were you told? (Probe)

(3) Did you join any social or other groups? (Formal or informal) (Probe) (Get names)

(4) In your off-hours did you tend to spend most of your time with other legislators? What kinds of things would you do? (Probe)

(5) Did you try to get home as much as possible? How often did you get home? Almost every week end_____

Every other week end_____

About once a month_____

(6) Did you spend much time with the press? (Probe)

(7) Which newspapers are important in your district? (List)
Metros:

Weeklies, locals, etc.:

(8) Was the press a very good source of information for you?

(9) Do you think the metro press does a very good job of informing the public about what happens in Sacramento? (Probe)

(10) Does the local press--in your district--do a very good

job of informing the public about what happens in
Sacramento? (Probe)

(11) Is the metro press in your area very significant politically? (Probe) How?

To you?

(12) Is the local press in your district very significant
politically? (Probe) How?

To you?

(13) Generally, how influential is the press in legislative
matters? What influence does the press have in
Sacramento? (Probe)

(14) Using this scale (Form V) will you tell me how important
the press is in Sacramento? _____

(15) Who are the important reporters? (Get names)

Last year we asked you to estimate the amount of time it would
take to be an Assemblyman. Now, after a year, will you
estimate:

(16) About how many hours per week did you spend on the job
while the legislature was in session? _____

(17) About how many hours per week when the legislature was
not in session? _____

(18) Did your health suffer any as a result of the work of the
session? (Probe)

Before you were elected to the Assembly, you were _____

_____.

(19) What has serving in the Assembly done to this previous
occupation? (Probe)

(20) Even with the pay boost, has it cost you income to serve
      in the Assembly? (Ask for estimate if possible)

(21) Have you been able to stay active in any of the local
      community organizations? (Probe)

(22) Which community organizations have you been speaking to
      in this last year? (Get list)

(23) How much time does this take per week? (In hours)

(24) Do these groups ever pay expenses or even provide an
      honorarium?

(25) Do you ever have the feeling that you are constantly
      running for re-election? (Probe)

Turning now to the kinds of things people ask you to speak
about at these meetings:

(26) Which issues are most crucial to your district? (Probe)

(27) Are there any issues which are unique to your district?

(28) Which issues are most crucial to the state as a whole?

(29) Who are some of the people who have contacted you about
      pending legislation? (Probe)

(30) Which organizations do they represent? (Cite names
      above)

(31) Do they come to you with a well defined point of view or
      do they try to find out where you stand and then argue
      their case accordingly? (Probe)

(32) To your knowledge, which interest groups are most
      influential in California at the present time? (Get list)

(33) Who represents these groups? (Use list above, get names)

(34) What makes an effective lobbyist? What kind of a person
      is he? (Probe)

(35) To your knowledge, which interest groups are most in-
      fluential in your own district?

(36) Who represents these groups?(Use list above, get names)

(37) In this session of the legislature, did you find yourself
      more involved in district or state problems?

      District_____   State_____   About 50/50_____

We understand that now and then legislators are asked to carry
bills for someone else, another legislator, an interest group,
or some pet bill of a constituent.

(38) Did you find yourself doing this very often? Yes_____
      No_____

(39) What usually happens to this kind of legislation? Do you
      sometimes have to kill it in committee yourself? (Probe)

(40) Do you sometimes feel that the problems which you are
      asked to solve are past solution? (Probe)

(41) How frequently in this last session were "impossible"
      requests made of you? Often_____   Now and then_____
      Once in a while_____   Never_____

This last session of the legislature is supposed to have been
the longest in California history.

(42) With all of these pressures, did you find it difficult
      sometimes to relax at the end of the day? Often_____
      Now and then_____   Once in a while_____   Never_____

(43) How tough will this (next) session be? (Probe)

Turning now to the legislative process itself:

(44) Is there a field of public policy that you are most
      interested in? (Probe)

(45) Is there a field of public policy that you feel that you
      have a good deal of knowledge about? (Probe)

(46) Using this form, how important do you think it is to be
      a specialist, an expert in some field of public policy?
      (Form V) _____

(47) Looking at the committees, which ones do you think are
      most influential? (Get list)

(48) You are on the _____

      _____

      _____

      committee. How do they relate to your district or
      interests?

(49) As a freshman, what was your role or job on these com-
      mittees? (Probe)

You may remember, we asked about the importance of several
legislative inputs the last time you were interviewed. We'd
like to go over that list with you again. After a year's
experience, how important are each of the following factors
in the legislative process—on this scale (Form V):

(50) Sectionalism of North v. South   _____

(51) Sectionalism of Urban v. Rural   _____

(52) Sectionalism of City v. Suburb   _____

(53) City Government   _____

(54) County Government   _____

(55) Local Businessmen   _____

(56) Local Labor Leaders   _____

(57) Local Community Leaders   _____

(58) Local Political Leaders   _____

(59) Political Parties   _____

(60) The Minority Leader   _____

(61) The Speaker, in general, not the
      present incumbent   _____

(62) Committees   _____

(63) Committee Chairmen   _____

(64) The Governor, in general, not the
      present incumbent   _____

(65) The Bureaucracy   _____

(66) The State Senate   _____

(67) The Federal Government   _____

(68) Interest Groups   _____

(69) Parliamentary Procedure   _____

(70) Seniority   _____

(71) Each legislator's own ideology _____

(72) How about your own ideology, where would you put your-
      self on this scale? (Form VI)   _____

Going back to the Speaker, there is a good possibility that
the present Speaker will have opposition in his bid for reelection next January.

(73) What effect would it have on your activities as an

Assemblyman if you voted for the losing candidate?

(Probe)

We have been told that the Assembly, like most groups, has its own unofficial rules, the <u>Rules</u> <u>of</u> <u>the</u> <u>Game</u>, things members should do and should not do if they want the respect and cooperation of other members.

(74)   What are some of the Rules of the Game that you found in the Assembly? (Probe)

(75)   How are these rules enforced? (Probe)

(76)   On this scale (Form V) how important are the Rules of the Game?   _____

We have been told that legislative work is done in many different places. How significant is the work that gets done in each of these places? (Form V)

(77)   The floor of the Assembly?   _____

(78)   The halls of the Assembly?   _____

(79)   The committee sessions?   _____

(80)   The informal social gatherings?   _____

(81)   The party caucuses?   _____

(82)   The Assemblymen's own offices?   _____

Now I'd like to read you several statements. Will you please indicate on this scale how strongly you agree or disagree with each statement. (Form VII)

(83)A The job of an Assemblyman is to work for what his constituents want even though this may not always agree with his personal view.   _____

   B The legislature is a full-time job.   _____

C Under our form of government, every individual should
  take an interest in government directly, not through
  interest group organizations.   _____

D The best interests of the people would be better served
  if Assemblymen were elected without party labels.

                                           _____

E The salaries of Assemblymen ought to be substantially
  increased.   _____

F I expect interest groups or their agents will give me
  valuable help in lining-up support for my bills.

                                           _____

G An Assemblyman can decide how to vote on most issues by
  asking himself if the proposed law is morally right.

                                           _____

H If a bill is important for his party's record, an
  Assemblyman should vote with his party even if it costs
  him some support in his district.   _____

I The legislature should meet most of the year, like
  Congress.   _____

J I will seldom have to sound out my constituents because
  I think so much like them that I know how to react to
  almost any proposal.   _____

K More staff and research facilities should be available
  to the Assembly.   _____

L I expect to get valuable help in drafting bills or
  amendments from interest groups or their agents.

                                           _____

M It's just as important to be on guard against ideas put
  out by people of one's own party as against ideas put
  out by people in the opposite party.   _____

N With his better sources of information, an Assemblyman
  should vote as he thinks best even when his constituents
  disagree.   _____

O Under our form of government, every individual should
  take an interest in government directly, not through a
  political party.   _____

P Interest groups have entirely too much influence in the
  California legislature today.   _____

Looking back over this past year:

(84) What are some of the more enjoyable things about holding
      public office? (Probe)

(85) What are some of the things you like least about holding
      public office? (Probe)

(86) Using these scales again, how would you rate holding
      public office? Form III_____ Form IV_____

(87) As of now, where would you put yourself on this achieve-
      ment ladder? (Form I)   _____

(88) What is the highest point on this ladder that you could
      reasonably hope to achieve?   _____

(89) Using this scale, where would you put yourself on the
      social class scale? (Form II)   _____

(90) Think now for a minute about the other freshman Assembly-
      men, the ones that are most effective. Why are they
      effective? (Probe)

(91) Who are they? (Get names)

(92) Now, how about the freshmen who are least effective.
      Why are they so ineffective? (Probe)

(93) Looking back over your first session as an Assemblyman
      what advice would you give to a freshman? (Probe)

(94) Was there anything that you did that you wouldn't do
      again?

(95) Is there something that you would do differently?
      (Probe)

(96) In this last session of the legislature are there some
      legislators with whom you have worked most closely?
      Who are they? (List five names)

(97) This is the end of my questionnaire. Is there anything
      that you would like to add?

Finish this part after the interview is over:

(98) Were other persons present within earshot during the
      interview? Yes_____ No_____

(99) Interviewers' estimate of respondent's frankness. Very
      frank_____ Frank_____ Not very frank_____
      Very evasive_____

(100) Interviewers' estimate of respondent's cooperation during
      the interview. Very co-op._____ Co-op._____
      Not very co-op._____ Very un-co-op._____

(101) Any other comments?

(102) Location of interview: R's home_____
      R's field office_____

R's Sacramento office_____

Other_____

(103) Time of interview: Time Began_____

                           Time Ended_____

(104) Date of interview_____

(105) Respondent's name:_____

APPENDIX D:

Legislative Socialization Survey
Schedule Number Three

This is the third interview in the series which we began in
1966 when you and others were seeking election to the California Assembly. This interview is considerably shorter
than the others--approximately twenty to twenty-five minutes.

(1) This is the start of your second term--do you have any
feeling that you are not considered a veteran now? (If
yes, probe)

(2) Do you think that the size of your class--those elected
with you in 1966--had any impact on the way you were
treated during your first year here?

(3) There are fewer freshmen this year--do you see them as
being any different from the class of '66?

(4) What are some of the characteristics of an influential
Assemblyman? What makes an Assemblyman effective?

(5) Which ones of your class do you consider most effective?
(Get at least three names)

(6) I'd like to ask you some of the same questions which we
asked before. For example, let's look at the "Rules of
the Game," the unwritten but important rules. What are
they?

(7) How are they enforced?

(8) Where would you place the "importance" of those rules
on this scale (Form V)   _____

As you probably remember, we have also asked about the
importance of several legislative inputs or factors. We would

like to go over that list with you again--using this scale
(Form V).

(9)   The sectionalism of North v. South   _____

(10) Sectionalism of Urban v. Rural   _____

(11) Sectionalism of City v. Suburb   _____

(12) The wishes of City Government   _____

(13) County Government   _____

(14) The wishes of Local Businessmen   _____

(15) Local Labor Leaders   _____

(16) Local Community Leaders   _____

(17) Local Political Leaders   _____

(18) How important are political parties   _____

(19) The Minority Leader (try to eliminate
      the "person")   _____

(20) The Speaker, in general, not the
      present incumbent   _____

(21) Committees   _____

(22) Committee Chairmen   _____

(23) The Governor, in general, not the
      present incumbent   _____

(24) The Bureaucracy   _____

(25) The State Senate   _____

(26) The Federal Government   _____

(27) Interest Groups   _____

(28) Parliamentary Procedure   _____

(29) Seniority   _____

(30) Each Legislator's own ideology   _____

(31) How about your own ideology, where would you put your-
      self on this scale? (Form VI)   _____
      How important are the places that work is done? How
      important is the work that gets done in these places?
      (Form V)

(32) The floor of the Assembly   _____
(33) The halls of the Assembly   _____
(34) The committee sessions   _____
(35) The informal social gatherings   _____
(36) The party caucuses   _____
(37) The Assemblyman's own offices   _____

Now I'd like to read you several statements. Will you please
indicate on this scale (Form VII) how strongly you agree or
disagree with each statement.

(38)A The job of an Assemblyman is to work for what his con-
      stituents want even though this may not always agree
      with his personal views.   _____

   B The legislature is a full-time job.   _____

   C Under our form of government, every individual should
      take an interest in government directly, not through
      interest group organizations.   _____

   D The best interests of the people would be better served
      if Assemblymen were elected without party labels.

                                              _____

   E The salaries of Assemblymen ought to be substantially
      increased.   _____

F Interest groups or their agents give me valuable help
  in lining-up support for my bills.   _____

G An Assemblyman can decide how to vote on most issues
  by asking himself if the proposed law is morally right.

                                              _____

H If a bill is important for his party's record, an
  Assemblyman should vote with his party even if it costs
  him some support in his district.   _____

I The Legislature should meet most of the year, like
  Congress.   _____

J I seldom have to sound out my constituents because I
  think so much like them that I know how to react to
  almost any proposal.   _____

K More staff and research facilities should be available
  to the Assembly.   _____

L I get valuable help in drafting bills or amendments from
  interest groups or their agents.   _____

M It's just as important to be on guard against ideas put
  out by people of one's own party as against ideas put
  out by people in the opposing party.   _____

N With his better sources of information, an Assemblyman
  should vote as he thinks best even when his constituents
  disagree.   _____

O Under our form of government, every individual should
  take an interest in government directly, not through a
  political party.   _____

P   Interest groups have entirely too much influence in
    the California legislature today.   _____

Q   In general my views on the important issues facing
    the state have tended to become more moderate and
    flexible as I have served in the legislature.

                                                 _____

Open:

APPENDIX E:

Legislative Socialization Survey
Veterans' Interviews

Our research project deals with freshman adaptation to the legislature. We interviewed people we thought would become freshmen legislators before their election to find what their perceptions of legislative service were--what they knew about the rules of the game--what they expected. We have just completed reinterviewing these freshmen to find if their attitudes had changed since they had become Assemblymen. Now as a benchmark we'd like to ask you some questions to find out how senior legislators (i.e., those who have been here a few years) compare with the freshmen.

(1) Looking back on your first term here, what difficulties or problems did you have as a freshman?

(2) Was seniority a very important factor when you were elected to the Assembly? If answers yes--in what way?

(3) What changes have occurred in the Assembly since you were first elected?

    a. Has it become more partisan?

    b. Has it become more research oriented?

(4) We've been told that the Assembly like all institutions has certain unwritten--but important--rules of the game. What are some of them?

    a. How are these rules enforced?

(5) Using these scales how important are these rules of the game? (Form V)

(6) In general do you think that the role of the freshman
     Assemblymen is different than that of the veterans'?
     In what way?

We asked the Freshmen how important the following factors
were in the legislative process. Now would you tell us how
important you would rate them?

(7) Sectionalism of North v. South   _____

(8) Sectionalism of Urban v. Rural   _____

(9) Sectionalism of City v. Suburb   _____

(10) City Government   _____

(11) County Government   _____

(12) Local Businessmen   _____

(13) Local Labor Leaders   _____

(14) Local Community Leaders   _____

(15) Local Political Leaders   _____

(16) Political Parties   _____

(17) The Minority Leader   _____

(18) The Speaker, in general, not the
     present incumbent   _____

(19) Committees   _____

(20) Committee chairmen   _____

(21) The Governor, in general, not the
     present incumbent   _____

(22) The Bureaucracy   _____

(23) The State Senate   _____

(24) The Federal Government   _____

(25) Interest Groups   _____

(26) Parliamentary Procedures   _____

(27) Seniority   _____

(28) Each legislator's own ideology   _____

(29) How about your own ideology? Where would you put your-
      self on this scale? (Form VI)   _____

We have been told that legislative work is done in many
different places. How significant is the work that gets done
in each of these places? (Form V)

(30) The floor of the Assembly?   _____

(31) The halls of the Assembly?   _____

(32) The committee sessions?   _____

(33) In the informal social gatherings?   _____

(34) The party caucuses?   _____

(35) The Assemblymen's own offices?   _____

Now I'd like to read you several statements. Will you please
indicate on this scale how strongly you agree or disagree with
each statement. (Form VII)

(36)A The job of an Assemblyman is to work for what his con-
      stituents want even though this may not always agree
      with his personal view.   _____

    B The legislature is a full-time job.   _____

    C Under our form of government, every individual should
      take an interest in government directly, not through
      interest group organizations.   _____

    D The best interests of the people would be better served

if Assemblymen were elected without party labels.

_____

E The salaries of Assemblymen ought to be substantially
  increased.   _____

F Interest groups or their agents will give me valuable
  help in lining-up support for my bills. _____

G An Assemblyman can decide how to vote on most issues
  by asking himself if the proposed law is morally right.

_____

H If a bill is important for his party's record, an
  Assemblyman should vote with his party even if it costs
  him some support in his district.   _____

I The legislature should meet most of the year, like
  Congress.   _____

J I will seldom have to sound out my constituents because
  I think so much like them that I know how to react to
  almost any proposal.   _____

K More staff and research facilities should be available
  to the Assembly.   _____

L I received valuable help in drafting bills or amendments
  from interest groups or their agents.   _____

M It's just as important to be on guard against ideas put
  out by people of one's own party as against ideas put
  out by people in the opposite party.   _____

N With his better sources of information, an Assemblyman
  should vote as he thinks best even when his constituents
  disagree.   _____

O Under our form of government, every individual should
take an interest in government directly, not through a
political party.   _____

P Interest groups have entirely too much influence in the
California Legislature today.   _____

Q In general my views on the important issues facing the
state have tended to become more moderate and flexible
as I have served in the legislature.   _____

Optional questions—depending on time:

(1)   What are some of the characteristics of an influential
        Assemblyman? What makes an Assemblyman effective?

(2)   Could you tell me who are some of the more influential
        Assemblymen?

(3)   What about the freshmen—are there any that you think
        will become influential in time?

(4)   Are there some that have broken the rules and conse-
        quently are not as effective?

Finish this part after the interview is over:

Were other persons present within earshot during the inter-
        view? Yes_____ No_____

Interviewer's estimate of respondent's frankness: Very
        Frank_____ Frank_____ Not very frank_____

Interviewer's estimate of respondent's cooperation during
        the interview: Very co-op._____ Co-op._____
        Not very co-op._____

Any other comments?

Location of Interview: R's home_____

   R's field office_____

   R's Sacramento office_____

   Other_____

Time of Interview: Time Began_____

                  Time Ended_____

Date of interview_____

Respondent's name_____

ABOUT THE AUTHORS

Professor Charles G. Bell received his Ph.D. from the University of Southern California in 1966. He has been on the faculty at California State University, Fullerton, since 1964 where he served as Chairman of his Department, 1970-1973. He has also been an Associate Editor of the *Western Political Quarterly*. He is currently Professor of Political Science, specializing in California government and politics. His present areas of research are political socialization, California politics, and political futures. He has published several articles in various journals, some with Professor Price.

Professors Bell and Price received support for most of their work on legislative socialization from the National Science Foundation (Grant 1870) and were State Legislative Fellows of the American Political Science Association (1969-1972).

Professor Charles M. Price also received his Ph.D. from the University of Southern California (1965). Currently he is Professor of Political Science at California State University, Chico, specializing in courses in state politics, regional politics, lobbying, interest groups, and the legislative process. He has authored several articles in various political science and allied fields journals. At present, he is engaged in research on the initiative process.

TEXAS A&M UNIVERSITY LEXANNA